What people are saying about *OPEN...*

"OPEN is a revelation. With an engaging wit and a clear mind Dave Price casts a penetrating light on how the new dynamics of digital culture are transforming not only how we work and play but how we think, feel and learn. He writes with a sharp sense of social history and theory. But he argues too from deep practical experience as an artist, parent and noted leader in educational change. From every perspective 'Open' will open your mind to some of the real implications of digital technologies for how we live and learn in the 21st century."

Sir Ken Robinson, world-leading expert on education and creativity

"There are lots of books about learning, but there are hardly any that manage to put the coming education revolution in a context that makes sense both emotionally and economically. *OPEN* is a tour de force that is by turns inspiring, shocking, highly entertaining, but above all practical. David Price combines the rare skill of understanding an institution without being institutionalised - a maverick thinker who can, through force of reason and humour coupled with long experience, make the job of re-booting education a fun one. He's just the kind of revolutionary the new world needs - one who's influence comes from putting the power to change things directly into your hands."

Mark Stevenson, author of 'An Optimist's Tour Of The Future'

"David has constructed a powerful argument for Open Education initiatives and disciplines, not just within Academia, but also within Enterprise. His insights and observations make this a must read book for decision makers and senior managers in understanding what is possible within their own institutions, and what is essential in supporting vocationally focused education and life long learning."

Alan S. Greenberg, Education Technologies Consultant
& ex Apple Education EMEA/Asia

This title is also available as an ebook from Amazon

OPEN

HOW WE'LL WORK, LIVE
AND LEARN IN THE FUTURE

DAVID PRICE

CRUX
PUBLISHING

About the author

Photo by Emile Holba

David Price is a writer, consultant, speaker, and trainer. He is a Senior Associate at the Innovation Unit, in England, and Director of Educational Arts. After an initial career as a musician, he worked in adult, community and further education. In the 1990s, he worked with Sir Paul McCartney in establishing the Liverpool Institute for Performing Arts.

He now consults with organisations and schools, and has led a range of ground-breaking, innovative, education programmes, which have successfully re-engaged learners in thousands of schools in several countries. He has given talks all over the world, and written extensively. In 2009, he was made an Officer of the British Empire by Her Majesty the Queen, for services to education. He lives in Leeds, England.

For speaking enquiries: educationalarts@gmail.com

Twitter: @davidpriceobe
Website: www.engagedlearning.co.uk

Contents

―――――

Introduction

At 3.00 p.m. on Friday 13th August 1999, I was stuck in the UK's longest-ever traffic jam, with a heart attack. To add further drama to the situation, not that I was particularly looking for more, I had my two young sons in the back of the car. I knew that I couldn't leave them while I went in search of an ambulance. I've never been quite so dismissive of Friday the 13th since.

My chest was tightening, I was struggling to breathe, and my heart was racing irregularly. In fact, it was beating so fast that I gave up taking my pulse when I realised it was over 200 beats per minute. Somehow, I managed to hang on for a further two hours, crawling along until I got home and was finally able to call an ambulance.

After the doctor calmed me down, she explained that I hadn't actually had a heart attack, though it bore many of the hallmarks of one. I'd actually had an episode of something called 'atrial fibrillation', and she said that I had better get used to such episodes because I was likely to have more in the future. And indeed I did. The real problem, however, lay in trying to establish an underlying cause. As I'd been a competitive marathoner for some years, and was still in training, the consultants misdiagnosed a condition known as 'athlete's heart' – a benign, temporary enlargement of the heart muscles.

Eventually, it became clear that I had a genetically inherited condition known as 'hypertrophic cardiomyopathy'. The doctor casually observed that one of the risk factors was 'sudden death', so I shouldn't really undertake any strenuous exercise.

By this time I'd discovered Google search, so I spent the next two weeks terrifying myself into thinking I was going to suddenly drop down dead; if you try searching 'hypertrophic cardiomyopathy' you'll see what I mean. Once the specialists told me that having completed several sub three-hour marathons, it was very likely that I was at the mildest end of the spectrum, I relaxed a little.

However, the atrial fibrillation episodes eventually became more frequent and because fibrillating atria can't pump blood effectively, I was told that the 'AFib' was likely to become permanent. It seemed as though I would inevitably follow my father in having a series of disabling strokes.

I don't declare my health history because I'm a hypochondriac. I'm telling you all this because what happened next brought me face-to-face with one of the most powerful learning experiences I have ever had, and one which embodies a set of social phenomena which is radically changing how we live our lives.

You see, I discovered an internet forum for fellow atrial fibrillation sufferers.

I know what you're thinking: 'Is that it?' Because it's a measure of how ubiquitous these self-help groups have become, that we barely stop to think how they have impacted upon the lives of, well, almost everyone with an internet connection. But imagine for a moment the fate of a frightened, newly-diagnosed patient before forums existed. Other than leafing through an out-of-date medical encyclopedia, the curious patient in the search of learning was entirely

2

dependent upon medical professionals. Opportunities to understand their illness from a fellow patient's perspective were often limited to snatched waiting-room conversations. Even obtaining a professional second opinion was frowned upon.

In my case, I was able to reduce the frequency of these episodes from almost daily to once a year or so, thanks to the generosity of people who had expertise and personal experiences they wished to freely share in order to gain fresh insights and to help others.

These small acts of kindness between strangers populate and enliven forums like the one I visited. They happen so frequently that we no longer find this phenomenon the heart-warming miracle it truly is.

What happened during my time on the Afib forum is just one example among billions. In isolation, we don't think of them as anything out of the ordinary. Collectively, however, they represent a social movement affecting almost every aspect of our lives. We're radically transforming how we communicate, share and learn from each other. In a nutshell, we're going 'open'.

The Open Revolution

Going 'open' is a social revolution that represents a fundamental challenge to the established order of things – one that cannot be ignored. It disrupts and changes, so things can never be the same again. But, as with all revolutions, there are winners and losers.

The winners are ourselves, happily connecting and collaborating through global networks of friends, colleagues and online acquaintances. We are powerfully motivated by the easy access to ideas and information, and the informality, immediacy and autonomy that it brings.

The losers are our formal institutions: businesses, schools, colleges and public services that are failing to grasp the enormity of the change taking place. Most dramatically, the losers are also governments around the world that are now confronted by citizens who will no longer tolerate secrecy and deception. The toppled dictatorships of the Arab Spring may provide the most graphic illustration of this, but there are plenty of others. The fall-out from WikiLeaks, and the 2013 revelations of government-sponsored internet spying in the United States and the United Kingdom, point to a more widespread culture clash.

These institutions are still governing, trading and training for a world that no longer exists, let alone a world that could be. They're bewildered by the shedding of compliance and the insistence upon accountability that now defines us as consumers and citizens. We want our governments and public institutions to be transparent. We expect a different set of relationships with companies we buy from, and invest in, based upon social and ethical concerns, not simply financial ones.

How did we get to be so demanding? The answer, I believe, is simple: we became much smarter learners.

Because information flows faster and more freely than ever, and because we are better connected than ever, the barriers to learning are being dismantled. We share what we learn instantly and, generally, without restrictions. How we learn, and whom we learn from, has been transformed. Our reliance upon anointed experts and authority figures has diminished, while our capacity to learn from each other has spiralled.

And it's just as well, because the world has never before faced such a complex set of societal, economic, political and environmental challenges. They're so complex that governments and corporations can't fix them alone. Instead, they will increasingly look for user-generated solutions. This is why learning matters, and why *how* we learn has to change.

Learning happens in three locations: in formal education (schools and colleges); in the workplace, and in our home and leisure time (let's call it the social space). While we've become smarter learners, progress has been uneven. In just ten years our learning in the social space has irrevocably changed, largely because it has become 'open'. We are now learning more from our peers than we ever learned in school. We're removing the intermediaries from every aspect of our lives so that we can directly deal with, and talk to each other in ways that have only become possible in the 21st century. We've even created our own 'sharing' economy.

Aside from some notable exceptions, however, learning in the workplace and in our schools and colleges remains static. The central message contained within these pages is that going 'open' in our formal institutions, will turn learning enclosures into learning commons, and significantly improve all our lives.

'Open' is a messy and at times chaotic phenomenon, but it isn't about to go into reverse. It has changed how we live and learn, socially. If we fully understand and grasp its potential, we can be more engaged and fulfilled in our work and studies, and better able to adapt to the uncertainties that we face in the future.

Chapter One

The State We're In

By any yardstick, 2011 was a pretty tumultuous year for social action. When Mohamed Bouazizi, a Tunisian street fruit-seller, set himself alight in protest at his scales being taken from him by an over-aggressive policewoman, few would have seen this apparently futile act of self-immolation as the first flowering of the Arab Spring. The public protest, which began on 17th December 2010, after Bouazizi's death, quickly spread from his home town of Sidi Bouzid to the capital, Tunis, and soon engulfed Egypt, Syria and Libya, eventually affecting almost every country in the Middle East.

In the UK, eight months later, on a hot August night in London, insensitivity shown by police in Tottenham, following the fatal shooting of Mark Duggan, turned a peaceful protest ugly. A crowd (mainly consisting of Duggan's family and friends) were refused a meeting with senior police officers. Hours passed and, with anger rising, the protesters refused to go home. Soon they were joined by a younger, more militant crowd, and by 10 p.m. shops, police cars and homes in Tottenham were ablaze. Over the course of the next four days the rioting spread to many cities in England. Claims for compensation in London alone exceeded £300m. Five people died and a traumatised nation looked for underlying reasons. The UK Prime Minister, David Cameron, had no doubts. Refusing calls for a government inquiry, he dismissed the riots as 'criminality, pure and simple'. The Guardian newspaper came to a rather different conclusion. In 'Reading The Riots', a report jointly commissioned with the London School of Economics, 85 percent of the 270 rioters questioned said that aggressive policing was an important factor in why the riots happened.

On 17th September, Adbusters, a self-styled 'global network of culture jammers', issued a call for people to march through Lower Manhattan to 'Occupy Wall Street'. Over 5,000 people responded. The anthropology scholar David Graebner, (who is credited with the totemic 'We Are The 99%' slogan) urged the protestors to set up long-term encampments. To the obvious frustration of press and TV, the emerging Occupy movement refused to conform to common stereotypes of organised rebellion – it had no leaders, no articulated 'demands'. In essence, it sought to model participatory democracy in miniature on each site. The speed of the global spread of the movement took almost all of the media outlets by surprise. By December 2011, 2,720 'occupations' were taking place in cities in over 20 countries.

In the spring of 2011, the global financial crisis was triggering contagion among Eurozone countries: first Greece, then Spain, then Italy and Portugal. Young Spaniards took to the streets as youth unemployment climbed throughout the summer to almost 60 percent. Over six million people – young and old – took part in marches and encampments. As their economy faced meltdown, Greece witnessed sporadic civil unrest. However, when a series of austerity measures were announced in the summer and autumn of 2011, the protesters intensified their demonstrations and protests and coordinated their actions with the Occupy gatherings that were being held globally.

Things Fall Apart

It seemed like the whole world was angry. But to see the protests in North Africa, Europe and the United States as a series of disconnected events, would, in my view, be a mistake. For one thing, we've seen this movie before.

In mid-19th century France, King Louis Phillipe attempted to reinforce his increasingly shaky grip on power by enforcing an already-established ban on public assemblies. Political activists, however, found an ingenious way around this. Dubbed the *'Campagne des Banquets'* (the banquet campaign) a series of meetings circumvented the 1835 law which banned public assemblies, by describing them as private banquets. It's perhaps only the French who would combine political agitation with fine dining, but its effect was profound. No doubt fuelled by some tasty wines, it's believed that the *'Liberté, Egalité, Fraternité'* motto was coined at one such banquet.

Their popularity quickly grew and pretty soon every province in France was staging banquet campaigns. The King felt decidedly uneasy about these social (though notionally private) gatherings and banned a large one planned for 22nd February 1848. In hindsight, this was not one of his better decisions. The resulting riot triggered the start of the 1848 revolution and the end of his reign in France. Passing the decidedly hot potato of kingship to his nine-year-old grandson, Phillipe, Louis Phillipe caught the next cab to London calling himself 'Mr Smith' (I'm not making this up) where he lived out the rest of his days. Back in Paris, the 'Second Republic' was proclaimed.

Throughout 1848, rebellions and revolts took place in Italy, Switzerland, Hungary, Denmark, Germany, Ireland, Poland, Belgium, and even Brazil. It was every bit as dramatic as the domino-effect witnessed in the Arab Spring of 2011, even if all of the uprisings were subsequently quashed. However, these popular rebellions eventually resulted, in most countries, in either constitutional reform or, in the case of France and Russia, in full-blown, bloody revolution. Like the global discontent seen in 2011, the mass demonstrations of 1848 appeared to have no through-line, no linking narrative; but look a little closer, and some striking similarities appear.

First, many of the participants in the uprisings of 1848 and 2011 shared a common demographic: a young middle-class, hell-bent on political reform, allied to a young (non) working-class, hell-bent on a better quality of life. The people on the streets in Tunisia, Egypt, Yemen and Syria were predominantly young, middle-class and well-educated, but they were soon joined by the poor, unemployed and uneducated. Similarly, the Occupy Wall Street protestors – two-thirds of whom were below the age of 35 – were a combination of employed graduates and the unemployed and/or homeless. This union, between the well-educated middle-class and the oppressed poor, was also a common feature of the 1848 rebellions

Second, the coalition of intellectuals and unemployed fuelled ambitions not just for a rebalancing of wealth, but for wholesale systemic change. Though rebellions in both centuries had specific political demands, they were primarily about the emergence of a broader set of philosophies; it's no coincidence that Karl Marx published the Communist Manifesto in 1848.

Third, the ideas behind these new social and political movements were able to propagate through the rise of disruptive, facilitative technologies. The mid-19th century saw the arrival of the popular press – European daily newspapers, like *Le Figaro* (France), *Corriere Della Sera* (Italy), *Die Frankfurter Allgemeine Zeitung* (Germany), were founded at this time. The growing numbers of literate middle-class Europeans were therefore able to learn about the protests with unprecedented speed.

In 2011, the disruptive technologies were digital, with social media and citizen journalism at the forefront, flat-footing both mainstream media and the police with their speed and agility. Before Mayor Bloomberg ordered the eviction of Occupy protestors from New York's Zuccotti Park, he cleared out the journalists, attempting to impose a media blackout. But I was one of 700,000 viewers who watched the evictions live, thanks to Tim Pool reporting on Ustream, using nothing more than a smartphone. Rioters in London were able to out-manoeuvre police riot squads by using Blackberry's private messaging system and the use of Twitter and YouTube in publicising the Arab uprisings is well-documented: the most popular Twitter hashtag of 2011 was #egypt.

So, having witnessed the confluence of factors in the late 19th century – a common demographic, a set of higher goals, the advent of powerful information technologies, and a reanimated counter culture – we should not have been too surprised by the events of 2011.

Eating Our Lunch

A sense of indignity was, and continues to be, felt by young people from Tottenham to Tunisia, from San Francisco to Santander. They did as they were told, worked hard, got a degree and yet, through no fault of their own, now have little chance of reaching the level of prosperity their parents enjoyed.

While the young feel anger at the loss of their future, the rest of us feel frustration. The after-shock of the global financial crisis is compounded by the dawning realisation that globalisation isn't simply an economic theory. It has costs and human consequences – and there seems to be nothing we can do about it. Government actions are outmuscled by multi-national corporate strategies.

When President Obama asked to meet with Steve Jobs, the late Apple boss, his first question was 'how much would it cost to make the iPhone in the United States, instead of overseas?' Jobs was characteristically blunt, asserting that 'those jobs are never coming back'. In point of fact, it's been estimated that making iPhones exclusively in the US would add around $65 to the cost of each phone – not an unaffordable cost, or an unthinkable drop in margin for Apple, if it meant bringing jobs back home.

But American workers aren't going to be making iPhones anytime soon, because of the need for speed, and scale, in getting the product on to shelves around the world. When Apple assessed the global demand for the iPhone it estimated that it would need almost 9,000 engineers overseeing the production process to meet demand. Their analysts reported that it would take nine months to recruit that many engineers in the US – in China, it took 15 days. It's these kind of tales that cause US conservative media outlets to graphically describe Asia as 'eating the lunch' off the tables of patriotic, if sleep-walking, American citizens.

If Apple had chosen to go to India, instead of China, the costs may have been slightly higher, but the supply of suitably qualified engineers would have been just as plentiful. While China may be the world's biggest manufacturing plant, India is set to lead the way in the industry that poses the biggest threat to western middle-class parents seeking to put their sons or daughters through college: knowledge.

The Myth of the Knowledge Economy
Ah yes, knowledge. Acquiring and applying knowledge in order to remain economically competitive is, of course, the whole point of the learning revolution. Yet here again, we've been wrong-footed. Part of the reason for the state we're in is our

failure to anticipate that, while the social value of knowledge would soar (as we'll see in the chapters that follow), its economic value would plummet.

During the 1990s a phalanx of futurologists told us that the 'knowledge economy' would follow the industrial economy, and we were set to clean up, because: a) we had the best universities in the world, and b) we spoke English, the universal language of knowledge. The rationale was that, in the future, knowledge would be at a premium, and could only increase in value. This was the doctrine that persuaded Tony Blair, the newly-elected UK Prime Minister, in 1997, to famously state his three priorities as 'education, education and education'.

The blind faith in knowledge, however, turned out to be misplaced. Thanks to the ubiquity of the internet, and the rapid scaling up of tertiary education in countries like Brazil, Russia, India and China (the so-called BRIC economies) the futurologists couldn't have been more wrong.

The first decade of the 21st century saw the balance of power in the knowledge economy decisively swing, from the West to the East, partly due to the eternal laws of supply and demand. Having a market flooded with BRIC graduates means that the price of knowledge has gone down, not up. These days, there is simply no point in paying $15,000 for a basic website (yes, that's really what they used to cost). Far better to either pay $500 for an Indian IT graduate to do it for you, or if you're prepared to teach yourself some basic web skills, get one of the free sites available online.

We all enjoy getting information at low, or no cost, but this simple illustration highlights one of the most turbulent social problems the West faces: the misalignment of professional skills to market conditions. If you are a middle-class parent reading this, consider the following statistic: of the UK graduates who left university in 2007, 28 percent of them were without a full-

13

time job three years later.[1] Clearly, some of the increase can be attributed to rising unemployment, and, in particular, youth unemployment, as a result of the sluggish UK economy. But, it seems as though the old axiom that 'learning is earning' – that, over the course of their working lives, graduates will always earn more money than non-graduates – may no longer be the case, especially given the rising costs of attending university.

Academics James Paul Gee and David Williamson Shaffer have warned against the dangers of assuming that the jobs that are disappearing in the US are simply call centres or blue-collar work:

> "It is a mistake – a potentially disastrous mistake – to think of job loss in America as only about the old manufacturing jobs. Many of those are gone already, and the assembly lines that are left are high tech, anyway. Now the scientific, medical, technological, and engineering jobs are starting to go too."[2]

The End of 'The Job'

Gee and Shaffer highlight the difference between 'commodity jobs' – standardised, replicable and sold at a reasonable price – and 'innovation jobs', which require specialised, unique skills. Because it's a relatively simple task to train workers doing commodity jobs, they can be sourced anywhere in the world. Gee and Shaffer argue that the US education system is still preparing students for commodity jobs, and thus facing overwhelming competition from developing countries, when it

---

1 Source: UK Higher Education Statistics Agency

2 Gee, J.P., Williamson Shaffer, D. *'Before Every Child Is Left Behind: How epistemic games can solve the coming crisis in education'* University of Madison-Wisconsin and Academic Advanced Distributed Learning Co-Laboratory

should be educating and training for 'innovation jobs', which are less easily outsourced.

In fact, 'jobs' is something of a misnomer: in the future, we are more likely to be talking about 'tasks' or contracts. Phillip Brown's book, 'The Global Auction', shows how companies can now slash costs by disaggregating what used to be a full-time job into a series of tasks, that can then be commissioned via a global 'reverse auction'. Banish any idea of eBay-style rising bids here – in these auctions, the lowest price for the job usually wins. The stark reality is that the middle-classes of the developed world are now in a 'high skills/low income' environment, and the prospects for graduates entering the knowledge economy are going to be tough for a long time to come.

If all this comes as news to you, then don't beat yourself up over it. I see no evidence of our schools, universities or indeed politicians talking about this unsettling future, this radical transformation of the labour market. In mainstream media broadcasts we only hear about Chinese and Indian workers stealing our lunch, triggering wide-scale job losses when the point surely is about the loss of 'the job'. The social forecaster, Paul Saffo, asserts that 'figuring out what will replace the job is the greatest challenge of the next 30 years'.

We've been hearing for a long time about how the future will require us all to have 'portfolio careers'. Our kids are less likely to be applying for jobs and more likely to be bidding for contracts. I speak from personal experience, here. At the time of writing, both my sons are in their mid-twenties, and both bid for IT-related contracts on a variety of auction sites. In order to try to understand how much the labour market was changing, I visited one of the sites they are registered with. I'd strongly recommend that you do too, because here's where you'll find the future, except it's happening now.

Shopping for Skills

Elance.com is perhaps the longest-established of many sites which specialise in 'Knowledge Process Outsourcing' (KPO). With over 1.3 million contractors registered by 2012, it had brokered almost half a billion dollars in contracts, taking a cut of between seven and eight percent. It posts well over 50,000 'jobs' a month and in a 2011 poll, 36 percent of contractors using Elance said it was their sole source of income. Every step of the process, from recruitment, to selection, to managing the contractor, and then paying them, is handled through the site.

The range of professional services being brokered is impressive – programmers, designers, researchers, marketers, engineers, managers, lawyers, journalists – and becoming more diverse by the month. But the power of such sites, and the foreteller of what lies ahead, is in the section that allows you to see the Dutch auction in progress. US contractors, pitching for legal work, will quote around $125 per hour; Indian contractors, just as well qualified as their American equivalents, are asking for $15 per hour. So, all things being equal, whose bid are you likely to accept?

The numbers are mind-blowing. In 2012, knowledge process outsourcing was set to contribute over 15 billion US dollars to the Indian economy, fuelled by an almost endless supply of highly-qualified graduates, willing to work for a fraction of the wages of contractors in the West. The 'high skills/low income' economy very much depends upon where you're sitting.

Whether it's Apple outsourcing technical and manufacturing jobs to China, or hundreds of thousands of small western enterprises managing contractors in India, these new employment structures are shaking up the knowledge economy. We're building flexible, virtual project delivery teams, made up of graduates working in several countries, linked only by a

16

broadband connection and a desire to keep their reputation rating high and our costs low. KPO is one of the key reasons why highly-effective corporations are turning bigger profits with fewer full-time staff. Our politicians, meanwhile, are either afraid to alert middle-class parents to the growing crisis, or they're simply not getting it.

Let me sound a note of caution in this bleak scenario. I am not saying we face a future without recognisable jobs. It's difficult, for example, to see how service economy jobs can be broken down and shipped out to the lowest bidder. No one is going to outsource the driving of a London bus to Elance – yet. Indeed, the kind of skilled jobs that countries like the UK and Australia once looked to migrant workers to fill – carpenters, electricians, plumbers and the like – are now likely to be sought after by unemployed white-collar professionals.   Elance, and other skills auction sites, however, represent only the vanguard of a hugely disruptive movement, a process known as 'disintermediation'.

In almost every form of transaction we make, social and cultural as well as financial, we're removing the 'middle-men' who historically have connected producer to customers, experts to novices. It's probably more accurate, in fact, to call this process 'digital mediation' because in most cases, we're replacing human intermediaries with almost zero-cost, user-generated, online connectors. Think TripAdvisor and LinkedIn, rather than your local travel or employment agencies. Because it's a relatively recent phenomenon, we're uncertain where it will take us, but it's already clear that business will never be the same again. If we already have surgeons halfway around the world remotely steering robots in hospital operations, then how long will it be before we are using Dutch auctions for a range of jobs previously thought to be 'indigenous'?

The End of Growth

So far, I've argued that we need to radically re-think how we learn and innovate at work, as well as reshape our education systems, in response to the seismic societal shifts now upon us. The new landscape demands that we unlearn our view of knowledge, traditional employment structures and any expectation of economic privilege.

The difficult but unavoidable truth is that we are in the midst of a global economic rebalancing, which will take decades to sort itself out. In the meantime, our sons and daughters are stepping into a debt-laden, terrifyingly competitive future. Can it get any worse?

Potentially, yes, but how we view the future depends on whether we can teach ourselves to think differently. Let me explain.

There is a growing body of people who argue that all of the above means we've reached a watershed. Instead of planning for the return of economic growth they are predicting the end of growth; that we are entering a 'post-growth' world and we should welcome it. Before I introduce you to one of their most articulate spokespersons, let me just allay any fears you may have that their model suggests a dystopian future straight out of the film, 'Blade Runner'. Their projection of life in 2050, *if* (and it's a whopping big if) we have the courage and social responsibility to think anew, is actually quite heart-warming. Their view of the future means we'll return to localised, community-determined decision-making based on shared interests and the common good.

To better understand a possible post-growth future, I met with Donnie Maclurcan, one of a team of seven people that make up the Post Growth Institute. Donnie lives on the Hawkesbury River, just north of Sydney and, despite only being in his early thirties, has already packed a lot into his life. In another life, he might have been a hedge fund trader. At the age of eight he was an art dealer, selling his brother's art works. By the time he was 10, he'd set up his first enterprise – an ironing business, charging 15 cents a shirt. He started trading shares when he was 12, and it seemed his future as an entrepreneur was already mapped out.

But Donnie also had a passion for sports and community service. He trained as an exercise physiologist and spent time working with Sydney's homeless. In 2002, at the age of 19, he became 'that bloke who ran across Australia'. Raising money for a sight-restoration charity, Donnie ran almost 4,000 kilometres, from Perth to Sydney. Averaging over 60 kilometres a day, and, running through some of the hottest, uncompromising landscapes in Australia, Donnie arrived at the Sydney Opera House 66 days after leaving Perth Bell Tower. A remarkable achievement, is it not?

That's not the half of it. Donnie broke his ankle on the fifth day of the run.

If you're thinking 'type A' personality, you're not wrong. He subsequently completed his doctorate and has written two books on his specialism, nanotechnology and its potential for international development. His epiphany, however, came when he was working with the homeless and hearing tales from bright, successful people whose lives had gone catastrophically wrong through no fault of their own, merely because of fluctuating economic circumstances. It gathered urgency when rooting through 'throw out' items Sydneysiders leave on the streets for collection, he found fourteen US dollars in coins. How disposable had our society become, he wondered, if we now throw money away?

So Donnie set up a social enterprise to support new not-for-profit companies in Australia. It's work that he passionately believes in and he is convinced we are heading towards a not-for-profit future. Citing a recent report by Deloitte[3], which shows a steady 75 percent overall decline in corporate performance since 1965, Maclurcan argues the relentless pressure on profits will prove unsustainable:

> "The for-profits will collapse because shareholders are demanding profit. Whereas, the not-for-profit model has desirability, sustainability, feasibility and inevitability on its side. This is an emerging international trend. My hypothesis is that 'for-profits' will become uneconomic over the next 40 to 50 years. Wouldn't it be nice to shift to a not-for-profit economy where purpose drives our primary outcomes, in terms of business?"

Organisations like the Post Growth Institute challenge us to redefine what we mean by prosperity. They argue that we should *aim* for, not avert, low growth. They advocate ditching our addiction to profit, by managing our assets – human, ecological, financial and communal – more responsibly. And this, according to Donnie Maclurcan, also applies to how we learn:

> "We'll need to see a bigger emphasis on asset-based economics that asks 'what do we already have?'. Just about all our approaches to formal education, across all subjects, promote a narrow way of thinking that reinforces our dominant economic paradigm. We need asset-based approaches to education – what do you already know, what have you got to share, what can we build on?"

---

3 *'The Shift Index 2011: Measuring The Forces of Long-term Change'* (2011) Deloitte Centre for the Edge

Donnie's hypothesis may seem far-fetched, even idealistic. But we need look no further than the phenomenal growth of the 'sharing economy' to see that our innate desire to share what we know is being matched by the popular will to share what we own. Companies like Airbnb (let out a room in your house), Google-backed RelayRides (peer-to-peer car lending), Lending Club (peer-to-peer loans service) and Streetbank (share your under-used tools and skills) could either be seen as confirmation of an age of austerity, or an altruistic and ingenious way around it. One person's apocalypse is another's Aquarius.

Cheer Up, It Might Never Happen

I've presented a broad-ranging picture of some of the economic, social, environmental and political turbulence which has shaped our most recent past, and will dominate our immediate future. It's important to set the context for what comes next in this book, and not just because the complex challenges we face will need to be addressed by those who are likely to suffer the consequences most sharply: the current under 25s.

The importance also lies in the inter-connectivity: social movements in the Middle East trigger concerns about our reliance on non-renewable energies; successful pitches by IT engineers in India provoke angst among middle-class parents in Hertfordshire; a butterfly flaps its wings in Manila, and a university professor rewrites her lecture in Texas.

We face a complex set of possible futures and no one can authoritatively predict how things will look in ten years, let alone by the end of the century. We know only two things for certain. The first is that we should learn to embrace uncertainty, because this age of uncertainty could become permanent. The second is that if all the old certainties are gone, then we have to be open to radical shifts in how we work, live and learn. That's why going 'open' is unavoidable.

With all the preceding 'end ofs' it might appear that we're also approaching the end of optimism. I don't believe this to be the case. As Ian Dury sang, we have reasons to be cheerful, one, two, three.

The first is the political and civic re-engagement of young people around the world. It may be troubling for authoritarian governments and disturbing for sectors of the corporate world, but the combined energy and ingenuity we witnessed through social activism in 2011 is heartening for the rest of us. It suggests that the global challenges we face will be met by people who care, who are smart, and who know how to organise themselves. 2011 also marked the point where many of these groups stopped being intimidated by their masters and began to appreciate the power of reciprocal learning and collaborative action.

The second is that we are at the start of a number of other transformations – all of which share the principles of 'open'. As my friend and colleague Mark Stevenson observed in his book, 'An Optimist's Tour of the Future',[4] it's not always easy to appreciate the significance of the current scientific leaps of progress in nanotechnology, robotics, biotechnology, solar power, bacteriology or agriculture. These developments are nascent, feel like pure science fiction, but could possibly lead us to an age of abundance, and cheerfully confound the prophets of doom.

The third reason is not only the subject of the rest of this book, it's the energy that fuels the rapid progress we can make from here. The opening of learning is transforming every aspect of our lives. It offers the promise of a more equal distribution of wealth, opportunity and power. It can close the gap between

---

4 Stevenson, M. 'An Optimists Tour of The Future' (2012) Profile Books

rich and poor, sick and healthy, strong and weak, and it accelerates the speed at which we solve intractable problems.

We've never freed-up, shared, and trusted ourselves with knowledge like this before, so we are still coming to terms with it. How do we ensure that its applications can improve our lives, while protecting ourselves from abuses of trust? How do our minds cope with the torrent of information coming at us from every angle, every day? How do we convert so much knowledge into socially productive wisdom? What can we do to close the gap between those who have access to open learning, and those who (still) do not?

The genuine democratisation of knowing is still being fought over. While it's deeply disturbing to some with commercial and political vested interests, it's wildly exciting to social and civic activists who, in the words of one of the protestors of 2011, 'have turned off their TVs, and entered into community with each other'.[5] Let's see what it looks like.

---

[5] *'Why I Protest: Olmo Glavez of Spain'* Time Magazine 26th December 2011

Chapter Two

So What Does Open Mean?

Andrew Ng is an Associate Professor, and Director of the Artificial Intelligence Lab at Stanford University in California. He's an engaging presenter, so it's not surprising that his courses are some of the most popular on campus. Machine Learning ('the science of getting computers to act without being explicitly programmed') attracts about 350 students per year. But when Andrew decided to open the course to the general public, over 100,000 people registered. Coursera administers Machine Learning, and a growing range of online courses, to students around the world.

Although a for-profit start-up, Coursera has, at the time of writing, offered its courses for free in its first two years of existence, and over 4.5 million students have already signed up. 'Classes' are typically 8-10 minute video lectures, interspersed with short quizzes, to test for comprehension. There are also question and answer forums, with an astonishing average response time of 22 minutes. This is attributed to having students scattered around the world – there is almost always someone online, 24 hours a day, willing to offer a response. With such large numbers, having academics assess student work became unrealistic, so Coursera instigated peer assessment. Tens of thousands of students graded each other's work. Many academics were horrified at the prospect of students assessing each other, but pilot studies demonstrated that peer grading at Coursera almost always correlates to tutor grading.

Daphne Koller, Coursera's co-founder, is convinced that Massive Open Online Courses (MOOCs) such as Machine Learning have the potential to 'establish education as a fundamental human right, where anyone around the world with the ability and the motivation could get the skills that they need to make a better life for themselves'.

A farmer in a remote village in Africa finds his small potato crop under attack from ants. He cycles to the cyber cafe in the nearest town and learns that the ants are repelled by scattering ashes on the soil around the potatoes. On returning home, he scribbles down the solution, and pins it to the village noticeboard so that his neighbours can follow suit. A whole village escapes a devastating drop in collective income. Colonies of ants have to look elsewhere for food.

In pubs all over England, small groups of people who share a passion for beer and philosophy gather to discuss modern-day dilemmas such as 'Can the use of power ever be justified?', 'What is the purpose of literature?' and 'Is "Why" a daft question?'. The 'Philosophy in Pubs' group may wish to plan a vacation to Seattle to meet the 'Drunken Philosophers', or indeed (for somewhere warmer) to Singapore where 25 members regularly meet at the Raffles Hotel. There are groups of amateur philosophers meeting in cafes and pubs in almost every major city around the world. Nothing new in that – philosophers have been doing it for centuries. But now they are no longer intellectual cliques, they're open to anyone.

It's not just philosophy. Anyone who wants to meet people and learn something new simply has to go to the meetup.com website, where every possible (legal) interest is catered for. Meetup enables over eight million users, in over 100 countries, to physically attend over 50,000 Meetups per week. Yes, you read that right – per week. Its founder, Scott Heiferman, had the idea of a global noticeboard, in the wake of 9/11 and, specifically, after reading Robert Putnam's account of an increasingly disconnected America, 'Bowling Alone'. Like many social entrepreneurs, he is passionate about harnessing global communications to build stronger local communities.

These examples are a fairly random, microscopic slice of a phenomenon which is radically re-shaping how we live, work and learn in the 21st century. You probably take part in a revolutionary act several times a day. It may not feel very revolutionary, partly because we're in the thick of it, without the benefit of hindsight and partly because in a relatively short space of time it has become almost second nature for us to learn differently.

'Open' is a disruptive force because in the places where we spend most of our waking hours – the office, school or college – it's been pretty much business as usual. It's often said that a time-traveller from the 19th century, beamed into today's world, would be bewildered by everything he witnessed, but would instantly feel comfortable in a school. Similarly, although the tools of the trade have changed, today's office learning culture has changed little since the 1960s.

Now, these two sectors are coming under intense pressure to radically overhaul their learning systems. The problem stems from the ways in which we learn when we have a say in the matter. We're becoming increasingly dissatisfied, and consequently disengaged, from the way we learn in the formal space, when measured against the open learning we do in the social space. It's why North London rapper, Suli Breaks says, in his viral video of 2013, that he 'loves education, but hates school' and why workers avoid office-based training programmes, but eagerly take part in weekly Twitter discussions with colleagues around the world.

It's too easy to characterise those contrasting experiences in terms of the presence, or absence, of technology: mobile phones being confiscated in school; Facebook banned in the workplace. I believe that it's more complicated, and much more exciting, than that.

The cause of our dissatisfaction lies not in being denied access to software or hardware but in being denied access to different ways of learning and different people to learn from. It turns out that our preferences for how we learn in the social space are the polar opposites from those enforced by our institutions:

Learning in School, College & Work	Learning Socially
Formal: When, where, how and with whom is pre-determined	**Informal:** We learn when, where, with whom and how we please
Individual: We demonstrate our understanding and skills alone	**Social:** We study and demonstrate our understanding in groups
Linear: Learners follow a sequential programme according to the 'curriculum'	**Non-linear:** Learners follow non-sequential routes according to interests
Just in case: Knowledge acquisition precedes actions	**Just in time:** Knowledge is gained as the task demands
Tutor-to-student: One expert, few learners	**Networked:** The expertise is in the crowd
Transmissive: Teacher transmits, (usually through lectures) students receive	**Experiential:** Meaning is made and shared by experience

I'm not suggesting that all the learning taking place in businesses and schools is defined by the list in the left-hand column. Nor is social learning defined by all of the qualities on the right. But enough of it is to warrant a radical reappraisal of how we do things.

Open learning is frequently, and in my view, incorrectly trivialised as people 'just chatting' on social media. My belief is that this perception misses the point: 'open' is not simply about technology, it's about behaviour shift as well.

In the 1980s, the proliferation of what became known as 'e-learning' saw our learning institutions take traditional face-to-face methods of teaching and learning, and digitise them. The promise it offered was only matched by our sense of disappointment in what materialised, as the novelty of switching on a computer replaced attending a lecture, and words on a screen replaced words on a page. E-learning in colleges and universities suffered the same fate as the 'interactive whiteboard' in schools: a quick hop from 'this changes everything' to 'well, that didn't work'. Digital technologies will no more solve the so-called 'crisis in education' than airbags will stop drivers from having accidents.

What digital technologies can do, however, is to dramatically accelerate the changes in behaviours, values, and actions, which then transform the way we learn and our capacity to learn. Most people working in learning have experienced one of those light-bulb moments when they realise the enormity of the change that is upon us. Mine was when I realised formal education could no longer look upon learning which happens socially as either inferior or complementary. Rather, it's a direct challenge to centuries-old orthodoxies, and simply can't be ignored. The light bulb went off in an unlikely, and unexpected, place.

In 2005, I took both my then adolescent sons to the WOMAD Festival of World Music in Rivermead, England. Since it was the first time either of them had heard many of the musical styles being showcased that weekend, I was curious to see which of them would grab their interest. It turned out that the band which had the biggest impact on my eldest son, Jack, was a group of Tuvan throat singers, called Huun-Huur-Tu. Tuva is one of the remotest parts of Russia, bordering on Outer Mongolia, and throat singing creates some of the most extraordinary sounds you're ever likely to hear. The technique is often called 'overtone' singing, because the voice manages to create several pitches at once. To western ears, where we were reasonably satisfied with just the one pitch at a time, it sounds both magical and, because the overtones come from deep in the throat and have to be forced out, quite painful.

Like many traditional forms of music, it's a lot more complex than it first appears. Conventional Tuvan wisdom has it that you would need to spend years of apprenticeship with an acknowledged master singing, gradually exploring hitherto inaccessible regions of the larynx and vestibular folds, before you could produce overtones. And there's not just one technique. A quick dip into Wikipedia reveals that 'the three basic styles are khoomei, kargyraa and sygyt, while the sub-styles include borbangnadyr, chylandyk, dumchuktaar, ezengileer and kanzyp. In another, there are five basic styles: khoomei, sygyt, kargyraa, borbangnadyr and ezengileer. The sub-styles include chylandyk, despeng borbang, opei khoomei, buga khoomei, kanzyp, khovu kargyraazy, kozhagar kargyraazy, dag kargyraazy, Oidupaa kargyraazy, uyangylaar, damyraktaar, kishteer, serlennedyr and byrlannadyr'. (Top tip: don't ever try to beat a Tuvan at Scrabble.)

So, imagine my astonishment when, a mere six weeks after the WOMAD festival, Jack asked me if I'd like to hear his kargyraa. "Sure," I replied, pretending I knew what he was talking about. He then produced a deep growling sound which, gradually, layered a sweet, melodic, whistle-like overtone on top. I could not have been more astonished. I knew that he'd not undertaken any trips to Mongolia in the previous six weeks. Nor, to the best of my knowledge, was he proficient in herding horses. How, I asked, had he managed to acquire a skill that takes years of mentored study? "Oh, some English bloke spent a few years over there, and stuck a bunch of free modules up on the net. I just taught myself by following them."

This was my introduction to the open learning phenomenon that is sweeping the globe. From years of face-to-face apprenticeship, to just a few weeks of online study. And in 2005, this phenomenon had barely started. If Jack wanted to further extend his Tuvan repertoire (though I think his interest probably waned once the novelty of being able to do something totally unexpected wore off), all he'd have to do is to Google 'Tuvan throat singing', and he'd have 1.5 million avenues to explore: YouTube tutorial videos by the hundred; overtone singing forums by the score; a regular Tuvan Throat evening in a pub in Darwen, Lancashire; someone in Australia looking for an online coach; and, of course, the inevitable Facebook Tuvan Throat Singing page. Don't take my word for it. Google it yourself.

Fortunately, there aren't any actual Throat Singing Schools in northern England. Because if there were, they'd have to be finding a new business model. 'Open' is fundamentally challenging teachers of just about everything.

One of the reasons behind MOOCs popularity in the US is that public investment now demands a better return, particularly in student achievement. It's not widely known, but of the 18 developed nations participating in the Organisation for Economic Co-operation and Development (OECD) assessments, the US comes bottom on college graduation rates. There's considerable room for improvement.

For example, in 2011, four-year graduation rates for the San Jose State University (SJSU) were just *seven percent*; fewer than 50 percent of their students graduated after six years. Despite these appallingly low statistics, SJSU sits mid-table in the national public university rankings. As performance indicators go, we're in a sea of low expectations.

The Governor of California, Jerry Brown, decided something had to be done. In January 2013, he announced plans to pilot remedial online courses, delivered by Coursera's rival, Udacity, at SJSU. Governor Brown was no doubt emboldened by a review of research, undertaken by the US Department of Education, which concluded that 'students who took all or part of their class online performed better, on average, than those taking the same course through traditional face-to-face instruction'.[1] If the pilot programme succeeds, open online learning is likely to be introduced in all Californian universities, and when it comes to education, what California does today, the rest of America does tomorrow.

Arthur C. Clarke famously said that "Teachers who can be replaced by a machine, should be". David Thornburg reworded it to "Any teacher that can be replaced by a computer, deserves to be". Around the world that replacement process is starting to happen, as more courses go online, and more video tutorials are uploaded. As the evidence accumulates that online learning at worst does no harm and at best out-performs face-to-face, more learning institutions and teachers will have to 'blend' their teaching. We will see more alternatives to lectures in large halls, via anytime, anywhere online viewings. But it isn't simply the

---

[1] *Evaluation of Evidence-Based Practices in Online Learning: A Meta-Analysis and Review of Online Learning Studies* US Dept. of Education, May 2009

303425

when and where of learning that's being transformed – it's the how, too.

Back To the Future

The aspect of 'open' that is the most thrilling is the nexus of old and new. Put simply, the incredible tools we now have at our disposal are bringing us back to ways of learning that had long been discredited. To fully explain this, I need to give a potted history of how learning is organised. As we don't have the space, it will be necessarily simplistic, I'm afraid, but you'll get the point.

As far back as the Ancient Greeks, educators have disagreed about how people learn best. The historian Plutarch's quote that 'The mind is not a vessel to be filled, but a fire to be kindled', neatly encapsulates two opposing views. Those who advocate 'didactic' instruction put the teacher at the centre: the best way to learn is for the expert to transmit and the student to receive, pouring knowledge into an empty vessel. Retaining this knowledge has always been a bit of a challenge, so rote learning – memorising and reciting facts, multiplication tables, and so on – usually accompanied didactic/transmissive teaching.

As Sir Ken Robinson has brilliantly observed[2] this method of instruction[3] was easy to measure – didactic teaching begat rote learning, which in turn begat paper-based examination. It became the dominant method of learning in universities, neatly side-stepping the tiresome reality that in real life we're usually tested by our competence in performing tasks. Since we tend to only value what can be measured, that's the way it's stayed, until almost the present day.

---

[2] Robinson, K. *'Out of Our Minds: Learning to be Creative'*, (2001) Capstone
[3] When I use the term 'instruction' it is in the American sense, simply to indicate teaching in its various forms. The British tend to pejoratively misinterpret this as 'telling students what to think/do'.

The main vehicle for this form of learning is 'the lecture' and the main tool for rote learning became note taking. Once schools became universal they fashioned themselves after universities. I vividly remember endless 'lessons' in my secondary school that consisted of the teacher copying extracts from textbooks on to the chalkboard. We were then instructed to copy this into our notebooks. It was never explained why we had to do this – I can only presume that writing down what was already available in print was believed to assist memory. Clearly, little had changed since Mark Twain observed that 'College is a place where a professor's lecture notes go straight to the student's lecture notes without passing through the brains of either'.

There have, however, always been advocates of more 'experiential' or 'active' forms of learning, where the student assumes the central role. John Dewey, Jean Piaget, Maria Montessori and Rudolph Steiner argued that the learner wasn't an empty vessel, but carried experiences and knowledge that should be progressively built upon with the learner's full and active involvement. With these approaches – broadly labelled 'constructivist' – it's the tutor's job to 'scaffold' experiences so that the learner can make connections, build confidence, reinforce skills, and apply knowledge to solve problems.

There have been some high-profile products of these so-called 'progressive' learning systems. For example, the founders of two of the most successful companies in the world – Amazon (Jeff Bezos) and Google (Larry Page and Sergey Brin) all attended Montessori schools. Larry Page credits going to Montessori, not Stanford University, as the reason for his success:

"I think it was part of that training of not following rules and orders, and being self-motivated, questioning what's going on in the world, doing things a little bit differently."[4]

Despite notable alumni, advocates of constructivist teaching have been outnumbered by those calling for more traditional methods for perhaps a decade or more, at least in the UK and the US. Striving to achieve a high ranking in international comparison tables, like the Organisation for Economic Co-operation and Development's Programme for International Student Assessment (PISA), has fostered a desire to get 'back to basics'. Using high-stakes accountability to improve basic literacy and numeracy skills has been the focus of those countries attentions.

While the popular debate on how best to teach continues to swing back and forth, its anchor point – the centrality of school as an institution – has changed remarkably little over the past 150 years. For even the biggest critics of compulsory schooling it was hard to see how else we could educate young people. Even though I didn't enjoy my school career, pretty much the only alternative to going to school, during 1970s England, was to be home-schooled – and this was virtually unheard of among working-class families. The only other place you could acquire knowledge was in local libraries, but they were as boring as school.

The Inexorable Rise of The Informal
'Open' is shifting the focus of attention from how we should teach, to the best ways to learn. It's no longer about traditional vs. progressive, didactic vs. experiential. Instead, it's about what

---

4   Interview with Barbara Walters on ABC's 20/20 10 Most Fascinating People, 2004

we can do for ourselves, how we can tap into the knowledge and expertise that is within all of us, but rarely mined. In short, it's about the rise of informal learning.

Informal opportunities to gain wisdom and practice new skills have mushroomed exponentially, and this alters not just how we see knowledge, but how we see the power relationships behind that knowledge. The hierarchy between teacher and students is being transformed through open learning – from vertically downward (expert to novice) to horizontally networked (participant as expert and learner). Arising out of a number of behaviour shifts: the desire for informality; the uncovering of layperson expertise; and a loss of deference for 'experts', we are finally witnessing the transformation of learning. It has to be said that some teachers and academics are appalled by these shifts. It's hard to appreciate the significance of the loss of deference, and the attendant rise of informality, because they've crept up on us gradually over the past thirty years or so. Back then, our definition of 'informal' used to be very different.

I was a mature student in the early 80s. Having never believed I was bookish in any way, I was pleasantly surprised to get a first-class degree and for a while toyed with the idea of an academic career. Having applied for a PhD studentship there, I was invited to attend an 'informal' interview at the Open University in England. The panel consisted of thirty or so of the leading cultural theorists in the UK at the time. The 25 minutes that the interview took were so horrendous I have blanked them out of my memory, but the thing I will never, ever forget, was the point at which I was asked if I had any questions for the panel. Suppressing the urge to ask the real questions that were racing through my head ("Where's the exit?", "Could someone just shoot me now?") I asked if it would be possible, during my PhD studentship, to sit in on some lectures. Cue much sniggering, and then finally one of the professors loftily declaimed, "We don't give lectures, *we just write books!*"

Oh, how they all laughed.

I'm sharing this anecdote, not as therapy (though I do feel much better now, thank you) but because it illustrates our changing attitudes towards authority and informality. If those professors are still working at the Open University, they will not only be much more accountable, but they will have witnessed a redefinition of 'open'. The Open University is, thankfully, now making its resources available to anyone, and, in 2013, even launched a collaborative learning initiative: Social Learn[5].

While there are some educators who see the rise of informality as a sure sign that we're all going to hell in a handcart, for many, shedding the responsibility of being expert-in-everything is not only liberating, it's radically changing the way they work. Encouraging learners to share what they know, and constructing knowledge together, subtly shifts our expectation of teachers and other leaders of learning: from giving authoritative answers to asking challenging questions; from the sage on the stage, to the guide on the side.

The best learning professionals appreciate the complexity of the dramatic changes we're witnessing, and the implications for how we structure teaching and learning. Advancements in what we now know, in technology, neuroscience, emotional intelligence, self-perception, and much more, are making thoughtful practitioners fundamentally re-evaluate their work. The imperative now is not to incrementally improve traditional models, but to rethink everything, to make it 'open'.

The public debate, however, ignores this complexity for a more reassuring simplicity, encapsulated in Ken Robinson's lament: 'we keep trying to build a better steam engine'.

---

[5] www.sociallearn.open.ac.uk/public

Whenever education is discussed in the media, politicians and parents alike inevitably retreat into a 'when I was at school' certainty, based upon little more than a nostalgic belief that, if it worked for them, it should work for everyone. They are apparently oblivious to the challenge to formal education that the rise of the informal presents.

Why, for example, should the end-users of formal education – students – be satisfied with attending a physical centre five days a week, using technology that, in many schools, is slower and more restrictive than the tablet or mobile phone that they carry with them (but are usually prevented from using) when in school? Why should we continue to group young people by the year they were born, to study subjects copied from 19th-century universities, when their passion outside school is to develop skills, learning alongside people of all ages, effectively organising their own 'curriculum'?

Open For Business

While the political pendulum swings between more traditional and progressive approaches to teaching and learning, there has been rather more consistency in learning at work. And it turns out that, without the political intervention we see in formal education, we view approaches to learning as less of a battle between the didactic and experiential, and more of a blend.

We have had forms of apprenticeship, for example, since the Middle Ages. Raw novices acquired skills by observing and mimicking master craftsmen over an extended period of time. Indeed, acceptance as a craftsman was to be labelled 'time-served'. Apprenticeships were overseen by unions and tradesmen's guilds and worked very effectively until the loss of heavy industry in the West and the accompanying decline in trade unionism.

The white-collar equivalent of apprenticeship is the internship. Internships have become quite controversial in recent years. At its best, an internship is the route to a permanent job. At its most cynical, an internship ensures a university graduate is paid little or not paid at all, given little or no training, and has little prospect of a job at the end of the period of internship.

Notwithstanding, the potential for low-wage exploitation, internships and apprenticeships are generally favoured by employers because they are classic examples of the value of learning by doing. Young people tolerate internships because it's becoming increasingly difficult to go straight from higher or further education to a job, without something in between.

As we've seen, the global drive to lower production costs has fuelled the growth of knowledge process outsourcing. This means we're not only seeing jobs disappear, but with them, the learning capital of an organisation. If a business is simply buying in knowledge, as and when it's needed, how is it going to grow its own bank of knowledge and expertise?

Learning at work is, in fact, currently facing a kind of perfect storm: increasing business complexity; a growth in knowledge process outsourcing; consistently lowered production costs and a revolving door of employees and interns – all ratcheting up pressure on CEOs and company functions such as learning and development for quick fixes. To cap it all, the rise of open learning is now causing some CEOs to wonder whether there is any point in trying to nurture organisational learning at all.

What's known as 'open source learning' – where networked learners collaborate to improve practices, prototypes and models – is making innovation happen far quicker than a company's research and development department can manage. As a result, some major corporations have begun to look outside the organisation for innovation (more of this in the next chapter).

But they are in a minority. Most companies still see learning and development as a synonym for 'training' rather than innovation. Indeed, one of the indicators of the weather-vane nature of learning in the workplace is the uncertainty of where it fits into the organisational chart. Is it a function of research and development? Human resources, perhaps? Or should it be Knowledge Management? Or, as is the case with some enlightened companies, is learning everyone's responsibility?

Wherever it is located, our understanding of how employees learn best has undergone significant revision during the past thirty years or so. Aside from some maverick organisations, the predominant pattern has always been that knowledge travels downwards: from senior executives, to more lowly staff, via training materials and courses. Sometime around the mid-1990s we began to understand that knowledge could be found anywhere within a company, but that it needed to be coordinated. Enter Knowledge Management. Knowledge Management became fashionable around the millennium, though it has consistently struggled to accurately define itself. That struggle continues, because with open learning, the very idea of managing knowledge becomes almost contradictory.

We are slowly understanding that learning in the workplace has to travel upwards, as well as down. And to ensure that learning flows in both directions, we have to work with a complex set of factors: human behaviour, supportive technologies, workplace cultures, personal motivation, employee engagement, to name but five.

The Informal At Work

A classic case of trying to stimulate knowledge growth is Xerox's Eureka Project. In the early 1990s Xerox's 20,000 customer service engineers were becoming more mobile, with more of them working on the road. As a result, technical know-how was becoming locked within individuals. By observing technicians on call-out it became apparent that when an engineer found a problem for which the manual had no answer, they contacted a colleague on a two-way radio.

The more unusual solutions were usually retold, and elaborated upon, at co-worker meetings. It was here that the Eureka moment arrived. Daniel Bobrow and Jack Whalen, of the Palo Alto Research Center, led a radical experiment in knowledge sharing: "It suggested to us that we could stand the artificial intelligence approach on its head, so to speak; the work community itself could become the expert system, and ideas could flow up from the people engaged in work on the organization's frontlines." [6]

Piloting the Eureka Project in France, customer service engineers were invited to submit tips through forum-based software. Few of Xerox's managers believed that there was any value to be gained from worker-produced tips and tricks. But the engineers – after some initial resistance – saw the benefits.

Gradually, the resource bank of solutions grew. Assuming that sharing professional secrets would need extrinsic motivation, Xerox initially offered CSEs a $25 incentive for uploading a tip on to the Eureka database. The workers rejected the offer. As one said, "this would make us focus on counting the number of tips created, rather than on improving the quality of the database." The incentive to contribute was simpler: workers simply wanted recognition, by having their name attributed to popular tips. By the time Eureka was rolled out across all Xerox countries in 2001, over 50,000 worker tips had been added to the database. Having now become a seminal

---

[6] Bobrow, D. and Whalen, J. *'Community Knowledge Sharing in Practice: The Eureka Story'* Reflections Magazine Volume 4 Number 2

example of a 'community of practice' the Xerox model has since been widely copied (pun intended).

The Eureka Project has become the stuff of legend in organisational learning because it was one of the earliest documented cases of the power of informal learning, shared and grown by the employees, not management.

The rise of the informal means that learning becomes harder to pin down, harder to manage. Michael Polyani was one of the early pioneers of informal learning. Until Polyani's emergence in the 1950s, few had challenged the dominance of what was known as the 'scientific method' of learning. This method is familiar to all scientists and relies upon a sequenced operation: asking a question; forming a hypothesis; testing and analysing; replicating under controlled conditions; being reviewed by peers. It is as objective a process for gaining new knowledge as we have yet imagined. In medical research it has led to many breakthroughs, while also keeping patients safe.

Polyani, however, argued that when it comes to learning, true objectivity is impossible, since all acts of discovery are personal and fuelled by strong motivations and commitments.

Rather than being disappointed by the inevitable introduction of feelings, Polyani argued that we should welcome human passions in the workplace, since they lead to imagining, intuition and creativity. His belief that 'we can know more than we can tell' led to the emergence of 'tacit learning': we learn, not simply by logical reasoning, but by observing, absorbing, tinkering, following hunches. Tacit knowledge may be hard to define but there's no doubting its existence. Think about how you recognise a person's face. Now, try to explain it. That's tacit knowledge.

The really important aspect of tacit learning, as any apprentice will tell you, is that it's almost a process of osmosis. You gain more insight from simply being around someone, and sharing experiences with them, than you would do by explicit instruction. There's nothing new in this revelation: it was, after all, Confucius who said *"I hear and I forget, I see and I remember, I do and I understand"*. Tacit knowledge is gained most frequently through 'action learning', working with others on problems, acting and then reflecting on those actions. That Polyani's theories took hold at precisely the time that 'knowledge management' was gaining momentum must have been something of a mixed blessing for learning officers. There's a limit to the amount of 'managing' of tacit knowledge that can be done.

The wisest course of action is to create the right learning environment, culture and context, which brings people together to learn from each other. The old joke that 'collaboration is an unnatural act between non-consenting adults' may have had its roots in corporations trying to break down silo mentalities. But if 'open' tells us anything, it points to a realisation that we have to understand how people learn when they have a choice (in what to learn, and who to learn with) and bring that into the places where they are required to learn.

Chapter Three

Why The World's Gone SOFT

I believe there are four, inter-connected, consequential values which now shape how we communicate, and what we do online and, increasingly, offline. They are **Share, Open, Free** and **Trust**. They form an easy-to-remember acronym SOFT. More importantly, Share, Open, Free, Trust are verbs as well as nouns: actions as well as values. The central argument of this book is that, if we are to make the most of 'open', we need to design formal learning around these values/actions.

I use the sequence 'SOFT' – and not FOST or TOFS – because each set of values and actions creates the need for the one that follows. Whilst the word 'soft' may conjure up images of hippy liberalism, the reality is that the actions of sharing, opening, freeing and trusting are starting to disrupt business models, marketing strategies and organisational charts around the world. In effect, life is already becoming a great deal harder for any leader who doesn't embrace SOFT.

We should be in no doubt that businesses, schools and colleges that continue with 'command and control' as their dominant forms of leadership and intellectual property strategies are facing extinction, possibly within five to ten years. Why? Because we, as consumers, employees and, crucially, learners, won't stand for it anymore.

If collaborative participation now shapes and empowers everything we do socially, why should we revert to unquestioning acquiescence when we work and study? And who knew that, having been relentlessly reminded that capitalism was only made possible by self-interest and a desire to acquire, we'd actually discover generosity and support for the common good, because of SOFT?

Before looking at each of these values/actions in turn, let's return for a moment to my irregular heart, as diagnosed in the introduction. Aside from the sheer relief of talking to people who felt just like me (which even the most empathetic doctors can't do), my initial reaction upon meeting fellow Afibbers was one of hope. Because here were many people who seemed to have controlled their condition, albeit through adopting differing strategies, when the best-received medical wisdom one could hope for was to slow the advance toward permanent Afib, not reverse it. How had they managed to do it? Not only that, if they were now well, why weren't they off this forum, living life to the full?

Of course, as I soon realised, once I'd begun to control my condition, the people who benefit most from the collective wisdom found on forums feel the greatest need to reciprocate. So there was Jackie Burgess, a retired nutritionist from the American mid-west, offering expert advice on diets or supplements to try, long after her Afib had stopped troubling her. Or Canadian forum-founder Hans Larsen, a former engineer who, after developing atrial fibrillation, devoted himself to researching the condition to the point where he has so far written six books on the subject. We now have a label for the likes of Hans and Jackie: 'pro-am', to denote people who are occupationally amateur, but with a professional level of expertise in their chosen field. Forums are full of them. Pro-ams always existed, we just didn't know where to find them until the internet came along.

During my annual check-ups at the heart hospital, I occasionally describe to the consultants the enormous database of users, condition triggers, side effects, mental and physical symptoms, and novel solutions people have found to make their lives bearable again. They politely listen, but they are yet to ask for the relevant website address. Let me be clear: I have enormous respect for these hard-working, dedicated, professionals who always have much sicker people than me to attend to. But, for a teaching hospital, they seemed remarkably uninterested in how patients learn.

So, let's now look at each of these values/actions in turn, along with some striking examples of how they help us get stuff done.

Share

In his book, 'Here Comes Everybody', Clay Shirky detailed the growth of sharing on the internet – from pictures of cute cats, to videos of brutally suppressed demonstrations. One of Shirky's assertions was that sharing inevitably leads to collaboration, and that online collaboration would, in the future, lead to collaborative action. The future is much closer than it used to be: within just two years of Here Comes Everybody's publication, the Arab Spring had arrived, its spread made possible by YouTube, Facebook and a large number of forums and messaging services.

Much has also been written about social media's darker manipulations, such as cyber-bullying, paedophilia, and the emergence of disturbing pro-anorexia, and pro-suicide forums. From time to time, there will even be a moral panic around the dangers of terrorist groups using the internet to recruit and radicalise young people. The UK government considered blocking Facebook during the English Riots of 2011, yet – without a hint of irony – celebrated the ousting of Arab dictators on its own Facebook pages. Social media holds up a moral mirror to ourselves, and we don't always like what we see.

But we delude ourselves if we believe that simply closing down such channels of communication will make the bad guys go away. Terrorists used to communicate by letter, but we didn't try to ban stamps; we teach our children how to cross the road, we don't ban cars. The blocking of social media sites in schools – the default position in the US and UK – not only inhibits learning, it does nothing to help our kids develop the digital literacy skills (knowing which information sources can be trusted, how to verify accuracy, etc.) they will need beyond school.

On balance, the phenomenal rise in sharing is overwhelmingly a good thing. And it's not all about posting photos of your friends drinking too many beers, on social networking sites, either. Take the unexpected growth of mumsnet.com and its subsequent spin-off, gransnet.com. Both have enabled mothers of any age (Gransnet has subsequently built a virtual 'shed' for granddads to meet in) to share their parenting tips, challenges and anxieties. And the numbers are impressive: mumsnet receives 25,000 posts a day from over 600,000 registered users. Employing 35 staff, they have become a political force in Britain, mounting successful campaigns to improve miscarriage care and preventing advertisers from using sexual images of children.

In 2010, the Outdoor Advertising Association ran a poster campaign that foolishly claimed 'Career Women Make Bad Mothers'. After intense pressure from mumsnet.com, they were forced to replace it with one that read 'Sexist Adverts Damage Us All'. Advertising associations are not the only ones forced to sit on the naughty step: during the 2010 General Election campaign, the Labour Prime Minister, Gordon Brown, committed a serious faux-pas – subsequently referred to as 'biscuit-gate' by a delighted media – by being unable, or unwilling, to name his favourite biscuit in an online mumsnet Q & A session.

The power of sharing, and its attendant feature, collaboration, lies in two characteristics: the speed at which knowledge is shared, and the capacity to support actions. Both can be graphically illustrated through the story of 'The Claw'.

Beyond.ca is a forum for performance car enthusiasts. It has a niche membership, with a fair proportion living around Calgary, Alberta. Shaun Ironside, a local car dealer, joined the forum when, on 26th March 2008, a young man took a Nissan Skyline out on a test drive, but failed to return. Ironside duly reported the theft to the police, but wondered if Beyond.ca members might be able to help. Given the market for modifying performance cars, he was fairly sure that when it was finally located, the Skyline would have been stripped for parts. He gave a description of the young driver who, naturally, had given false ID: 'Distinguishing features on him were he was missing his ring finger and middle finger on his left hand... also had severe scarring on the top of his left hand. Light-colored, short spiked hair'. Ironside's first post was timed 10.24 p.m. 26th March 2008 (the chronology here is quite important). Several posters immediately offered commiserations, and promised to look out for the car.

By chance the forum's moderator pulled up alongside the Nissan Skyline at a set of lights the next day. Whipping out his mobile phone, he took a photo clearly showing the driver with the missing digits. He called the police, who said they would follow it up in due course. The photograph was posted on the forum at 4.19 p.m. 27th March, with the message 'I

FOUUUNNND THEM =)' (the driver had a passenger). At this point the story went viral.

Forums frequently propagate internet 'memes': images, videos or phrases which become manipulated and then spread rapidly and repeatedly. This is a classic case. Within a few hours of the photo appearing, hundreds of photo-shopped versions appeared – the most popular being a distorted road sign that labelled the thief, somewhat cruelly given his missing fingers, as 'The Claw'.

It only took five hours to find The Claw's Facebook page and the thief was identified as James Jacobson. By now, the thread had spread to forums all around the world. Even the Everton Football Club Supporters site in Liverpool, UK was following it.

Within an hour, forum members had tracked down Jacobson's employer. An hour later, and The Claw's home address appeared with the relevant Google map. Another poster, Numi, claimed to have seen the car parked at Jacobson's home, and once again, members were urged to call the police.

All of this amateur detective work had occurred less than thirty hours after the original theft was reported. With momentum building, around 2.00 a.m. 28th March, Jordan Andrew posted to propose that members meet at a garage close to Jacobson's house. One poster summed up the gathering excitement, *"Shit, I didn't think this would blow up to be this big"*. Guest posts arrived from the US, UK, Australia, and Europe, all expressing support.

Around 2.30 a.m., nine members duly arrived at Jacobson's house, but with no sign of the Skyline, assumed Jacobson had taken flight and left, somewhat deflated. A few hours later, though, another eagle-eyed member noticed the car back on Jacobson's drive and parked in front of it. With excitement running at fever pitch once again, the police were called.

By 8.00 a.m., Jacobson's employer had been called by several posters to inform him that Jacobson wouldn't be coming in to work today. The car's owner and the police arrived, Jacobson was woken and arrested. Of course, the whole proceedings were captured on mobile phones by Beyond members and immediately posted to YouTube.

So, less than 36 hours after the owner's original post, a group of enthusiasts, acting together, had shared their observations, skills, knowledge, intuition and social networking expertise, to track down, apprehend and comprehensively document the arrest of a car thief. Their motivation and collaborative actions ensured that the owner's car was returned to him, in pristine condition, before the car could be stripped of valuable parts. Better yet, the owner discovered that the Claw had left $22 and his baseball cap on the back seat of the car. Such was the notoriety of the incident by now (over one million page views in two days) that Ironside subsequently auctioned the cap on eBay, collecting $225 from the sale.

Inevitably, Canadian TV stations featured the story and a police spokesman appeared to solemnly remind the general public that they should not be encouraged by the work of Beyond.ca to take the law into their own hands. This conveniently overlooked the fact that, despite repeated phone calls requesting help, they had played no part at all in the tracking-down of Jacobson. Left to the police machinery to grind into action, it's more than likely that the car would have been dismantled by the time they'd located Jacobson.

I've laid out the sequence of events here in some detail because I believe it shows how quickly sharing can lead to collaborative action, and how empowering the creation of shared knowledge can be. Here was a group of learners, without direction or coordination, undertaking sophisticated detection work and making it look easy. They acted purposefully, in order to right a wrong, and were motivated by the support of others watching around the world.

Two final conclusions can be drawn:

1. Souped-up car fanatics require little or no sleep.

2. If the cluetrain stops anywhere near Calgary, the destination isn't police headquarters. The police spokesman clearly did not grasp the key issue here, and one which forms a central tenet of this book: that people will collectively act to determine their own destinies simply because they now can. The institutions, which are there to govern, protect, or indeed, educate us, cannot compete against the cognitive surplus of a passionate group of individuals acting in concert.

So the attraction of sharing to enable collaboration in the social space is clear. But what are the implications for business and education?

Collaboration and Innovation

Increasingly, organisations are turning to collaboration in order to accelerate innovation. If they needed any encouragement, a recent study provides confirmation. The Future Foundation surveyed 3,500 employees in companies in the UK, France, Germany, Japan and the USA. They found an 81 percent correlation between collaboration and innovation. UK employees who collaborated were twice as likely to have contributed new ideas to their company, compared with those who had not.

Sebastien Marotte is Vice-President of Google Enterprise in Europe, the Middle East and Africa. In responding to the study, he views greater collaboration as an inevitability:

"The speed at which ideas can be generated, tested and brought to fruition is accelerating faster than we could have anticipated – largely because of the explosion of social media and mobile and cloud computing. Over the next decade, the process of sharing and developing ideas will be dramatically accelerated by the advance of these relatively young technologies having a major impact on the way products and services are brought to market, businesses are structured, job roles are created and talent is attracted, rewarded and retained....For most people, communicating and collaborating in an online world have become the norm – organising a party, sharing news and views or coming together to fundraise is commonplace. For many of us though, cooperating this smoothly in our professional lives is more of an ideal than a reality."[1]

Marotte sees the pool of collaborators widening dramatically in the near future, moving well beyond employees. The buzzword for this is 'crowdsourcing': finding new ideas, new products, from anyone, and anywhere. One novel experiment in crowdsourcing was instigated in 2011, when the *New York Times* ran a campaign to invite readers to attempt to fix the deficit in New York City's budget. Creating an online budget simulator, they sought a wide range of options. They received 7,000 submissions in a week.

An increasing number of large corporations, including Dell, Kraft, Fiat, Unilever, BMW, Nokia and Philips have instigated crowdsourcing initiatives. Some appear to be attempts at genuine collaboration, while others appear to be little more than marketing strategies in search of a bandwagon to jump on. Starbucks, for example, invited customers to suggest new

---

[1] www.bbc.co.uk/news/business-16858085

products, services, or areas where the customer experience could be improved. Launched in 2009, 'My Starbucks Idea' had received over 115,000 suggestions by its second anniversary – yet only 150 were actually implemented.

Perhaps the most impressive use of crowdsourcing is to be found in an initiative by Proctor & Gamble. Despite employing over 9,000 staff in research and development, P&G were struggling to match the levels of innovation of their competitors. Their solution has been the creation of 'Connect and Develop'. External innovators and entrepreneurs are invited to pitch their product ideas, or solutions to P&G's technical processes, to a development team. If their idea takes off, they are rewarded with a partnership agreement. Launched in 2006, Connect and Develop has resulted in over 1,000 externally-sourced innovations. That's over half of all new product initiatives, generating over $20 billion of revenue income. Proctor & Gamble have turned the 'Not Invented Here' syndrome on its head: 'Proudly Found Elsewhere' is their new company mantra.

Do these invitations to collaborate lay down a marker for how business will be done in the future? Or do they emerge out of frustration with the inability of companies to establish internal innovative learning environments? If going 'open' is indeed irreversible then crowdsourcing is likely to become the norm – but that doesn't let companies off the hook in creating open learning environments. The most successful organisations are doing both.

*****

If collaboration is a headache for learning in the workplace, it's hard to know where to start with schools. First, most schools don't call it 'sharing' anyway – they call it 'cheating'. Think about it for a moment: the kids who are now in school will be entering a workplace where internal and external collaboration *is* the work. We prepare them for this interconnected world, by insisting that almost everything they do, every piece of work they submit, is their own work, not the fruits of working with others, because every student has to have an individual, rigorously assessed, accountable grade – if they don't, the entire examinations system collapses like a deck of cards.

Except it doesn't. Almost 20 years ago, I successfully argued with a validating university, that, in our working lives we were constantly being assessed on two simultaneous levels: How we performed as part of a team, and our individual contribution to the project in hand. They allowed us to award individual and group grades. It cannot be beyond the wit of our school examinations boards to do the same.

Similarly, the world doesn't come to an end for schools if we allow students access to the social media tools they use so prolifically when they're out of school. At the time of writing there are 400 million tweets posted daily on Twitter, 100 hours of video being uploaded to YouTube every minute, and over a billion Facebook users. For many professionals these have become absolutely essential learning tools yet most of our schools and universities prohibit their use.

Whilst a systemic obsession with testing deprives our students of the opportunity to learn the much-needed skills of collaboration, there are few such blockages to teachers working more collaboratively. Teaching, however, remains one of the most private professions. Schools and colleges have the freedom to arrange teachers' and lecturers' workloads so that teaching and learning can become a shared activity, but rarely exercise that freedom.

Those schools that are 'de-privatising' the process of teaching and learning – by knocking down classroom walls, teaming up teachers to work together, or taking the learning into the community or the workplace – are among some of the leading-edge schools internationally. However, until such spaces and such values and actions become the norm, schools will continue to foster cultures of containment, not collaboration. Sharing is another example where learning in the worlds of work and education trails behind the social space.

Open

This could get confusing, so let's try to draw some distinctions between the titular *Open*, as a defining movement, and 'open' as it applies to actions and values that support the exchange of information, knowledge and skills.

Going 'open' has become a global phenomenon, cultivated in the petri-dish social movements of the internet, but now also affecting our national and global institutions. Opening up the inner workings of governments could be seen as a mark of maturing democracies. Flattening company hierarchies and working with 'frenemies' – collaborating with companies who would normally be considered as rivals – is now a relatively commonplace feature of knowledge-driven industries. Open source, open information, open government, open systems, open organisations – it feels as though opening up has been the defining theme of the 21st century.

It's not that simple, of course. We may have corporations and governments beginning to realise that it's simply easier to adopt 'radical transparency' strategies, but we still have repressive regimes; we may have open source and open innovation, but non-disclosure agreements are still routinely deployed to intimidate legitimate 'whistleblowing'. We may have Creative Commons (a licensing system which encourages free sharing), but we also have attempts to impose legislative shackles on digital copyright.

Being 'open', in the context of values and actions appeals to people's sense of altruism and encourages reciprocity. Sharing requires us to be open, so we do it. Ten years ago that usually meant exposure to a small number of colleagues, friends or family. Now, being 'open' is a very public activity. One of the remarkable features of the past ten years is how rapidly we have adjusted to being 'open', especially those under the age of 30.

We are all still adjusting to the new demands and responsibilities that being 'open' presents. Employees get fired, marriages are broken, and lives are put at risk, because of Facebook indiscretions, which forget the world is watching and that actions have consequences. On balance, however, it seems enough of us feel that the benefits of being 'open' outweigh the attendant loss of privacy. In the personal story with which I began this chapter, if I wanted to access the wisdom of the crowd on the AFib forum, I needed to be willing to disclose quite personal details, in a very public forum. I got over it, more data was added, and I was able to make the connection between my digestive problems and my irregular heart rhythm (it's stronger than you might think) and thus put a potentially disabling health condition back in its box. In my case, the trade-off, between a minor loss of privacy set against making a cognitive breakthrough, was worth making.

The advent of social media has played a crucial role in opening up knowledge and information. Whistleblowing, in a pre-internet age, was more often than not tinged with disloyalty -- now it's seen as an inevitable response to 'covering up'. In May 2011, Ryan Giggs, soccer star of Manchester United and Welsh national hero, sought anonymity through privacy laws that allowed him to prevent newspapers from disclosing marital infidelities. 75,000 people took to Twitter to name him. What was he going to do – take them all to court?

When the UK's Daily Telegraph exposed the expenses fraud of hundreds of British members of parliament, the initial focus was on the hunt for the source of the leak. Politicians were left in no doubt about the inappropriateness of this response by the public's response on Twitter and innumerable forums. Suitably shamefaced, their energies became redirected to dealing with those who had falsely claimed, together with ensuring that it couldn't happen again. As author and innovation expert, Charles Leadbeater has noted:

> "Social media is creating the conditions for the emergence of a civic long tail, a mass of loosely connected, small-scale conversations, campaigns and interest groups, which might occasionally coalesce to create a mass movement. From now on, governments everywhere will have to contend and work with this civic long tail."[2]

The openness of our social interactions has persuaded many industry sectors to seize the chance to talk more to us than to each other. There was a time when business-to-business relationships were the only thing that mattered. Not anymore. Increasingly, business-to-customer relationships are paramount, and since we're content to reveal all in our online friendships, giving lots of personal information away to businesses doesn't seem to phase us anymore. A good example of this, and of the trade-off between user-benefits and loss of privacy, is the customer loyalty scheme.

Tesco, the UK retail giant, has the world's most successful customer loyalty scheme. The basis of all such schemes is a simple contract: shop regularly with us and we'll give you some of your money back. But the real value of the Tesco scheme was

---

2 Leadbeater, C. 'The Civic Long Tail' (2011) Demos

the mass of data, which Tesco was able to gain on the habits, tastes and spending patterns of their shoppers.

Dunnhumby were the marketing company who helped Tesco analyse the first set of data in 1994. After the submission of their first quarterly report, the then Tesco chairman Lord MacLaurin observed: "What scares me about this is that you know more about my customers after three months than I know after 30 years". Armed with so much 'big data',[3] Tesco were then able to establish stock patterns, and target special offers, personalised to individual customer profiles, which gave them the lion's share of the UK supermarket sector, which they still hold. Where Tesco led, Amazon, Google and the like, followed. Working with big data has become the Holy Grail of corporations, and with good reason. McKinsey have estimated that retailers using big data's full potential could increase their operating margins by 60 percent. We are no longer surprised by sidebar ads and recommendations that purr 'if you liked that, you might like this....' Was our privacy pilfered, or did we give it away?

Of course, none of this seems to unduly bother us while we're filling our supermarket trolley, or claiming our 'free' customer reward trip to a theme park. Because we want stuff, we've opened up. It's hard to imagine, despite the protestations of data protection groups, that we'll ever reverse the tide of being 'open'. Perhaps the best we can hope for is that if we've opened up, then our public institutions should too.

We have seen how collaboration and crowdsourcing is making businesses more 'open'. For many, though, that's not nearly open enough. Innovative companies are opening up all aspects of their operations.

---

[3] Big data is defined by McKinsey's Global Institute as 'datasets whose size is beyond the ability of typical database software tools to capture, store, manage and analyse'.

Many CEOs blog and tweet, though most are careful about what they choose to disclose. Some, however, have adopted a corporate strategy of 'radical transparency', encouraging any employee to go public on issues they care about. Some see it as easier than dealing with a constant stream of rumour and gossip, while others see it as good for business and customer loyalty.

Tony Hsieh, CEO of online shoes retailer, Zappos, is a prime example. Zappos has a companywide wiki, so employees can list complaints and concerns and air their grievances with Zappos; sales agents are encouraged to point customers towards competitor stores if they can't find the shoes they need; suppliers get to see all the financial information on the products they supply, including profit margins. Hsieh argues that the more customers and suppliers know about Zappos – good and bad – the more likely they are to do business with them. It seems to be working: in 2001 Zappos' gross merchandise sales were $8.6m; by 2008 the figure was over $1bn and the company was in the top 25 of Fortune's 'Best Companies To Work For' list.

Clive Thompson, of *Wired* magazine, advocates radical transparency:

> "Transparency is a judo move. Your customers are going to poke around in your business anyway, and your workers are going to blab about internal info – so why not make it work for you by turning everyone into a partner in the process and inviting them to do so?"[4]

Transparency's Unwanted Side-Effects

Schools and colleges are now being held to account by government demands for ever more open data. It's here, I believe, that the desire for information on the academic

---

[4] Wired Magazine, March 2007

performance of students becomes counter-productive. Successive English governments have deemed it necessary to publish data on the performance of schools in standardised national tests, claiming parents have a 'right to know'. This may or may not be the case. But education expert, Yong Zhao, refers to the need to consider education innovations in the same way as the medical community views clinical trials. The innovation may be successful on its own terms, but what about the side effects?

In this case, there's no doubt that introducing the publication of school league tables has influenced parents in making their (very limited) choice of school for their children. Here, however, is a case of data determining dialogue. Because there's inaccurate, or no, measuring of many of the things, which ought to matter to parents – the learning environment, incidence of bullying, scope for parental involvement, making learners confident and curious – the yardstick of what makes a 'good' school becomes distorted, the dialogue impoverished.

Since these aspects of learning are neither valued, nor discussed, schools have little incentive to become the kind of learning commons described elsewhere. That's why 'open' is dependent upon context – government's insistence on openness has led to schools becoming enclosed, overly focused on data and test results. So, the side effect may be that perfectly good schools get shut down, simply because we're told we have a right to know.

*****

Socially, 'open' is a more complex value and action than share. It is also politically and commercially contentious. In reality, it marks a battle being fought for the control of knowledge.

Governments vs. Wikileaks and US National Security Agency whistleblower, Edward Snowden; corporations vs. Anonymous.

But it also marks a fork in the road for how businesses should operate. Nowhere do we see this battle more clearly than in Apple vs Google. Apple profited hugely through Steve Jobs' insistence on secrecy and closed source codes. There are already signs, however, of customers frustrations at being 'locked-in' to Apple products and the company may be forced to open up more.

Google have an unambiguous position on going 'open'. They believe 'open' will eventually triumph over closed. In an email to all staff in 2009, Jonathan Rosenberg, Senior Vice-President, Product Management, spelled out the inevitability of open everything – systems, platforms, sources – and the ways in which it will change politics, culture, technology, indeed every aspect of our lives:

"It is counterintuitive to people who are stuck in the old MBA way of thinking, but if we do our jobs then soon it won't be. Our goal is to make 'open' the default. People will gravitate towards it, then they will expect and demand it and be furious when they don't get it. When 'open' is intuitive, then we have succeeded...'Open' will win. It will win on the internet and will then cascade across many walks of life: The future of government is transparency. The future of commerce is information symmetry. The future of culture is freedom. The future of science and medicine is collaboration. The future of entertainment is participation. Each of these futures depends on an 'open' Internet."

Free

For companies like Google, being open also means being free. As we'll see however, there are several interpretations to this seemingly innocuous word. Most of them apply to SOFT, so let's look at them in turn:

Free as Value

On 22nd February, 2010, US student Dan Brown uploaded a six-minute *'Open Letter To Educators'* to his YouTube channel. The video shows an extremely articulate, hyperactive, opinionated young man whose parting shot is 'I dropped out of college because it was interfering with my education!' The video has been seen by over 270,000 people and has triggered an extraordinary response – over 6,000 comments. Most of the comments are evenly split between young people either in, or about to enter, college applauding his argument, and older college graduates who are essentially chastising Dan for biting the hand that has fed him.

Their rationale seems to be 'if college did nothing for you, how did you get to be so smart?' This seems to ignore Brown's capacity for self-learning, and his argument that he didn't need books or lectures on his course, as everything he did need was available online.

For me, the key point in his argument is not whether the particular college he attended failed him or not. Rather, it's the eloquent summation of the bind all tertiary education now finds itself in: the value of knowledge, in the brave new knowledge economy of the future, was supposed to go up, not drop to virtually zero. So, given the high skills/low income future facing graduates looking for knowledge jobs in the developed world, why should an autodidact like Dan pay for college tuition, especially when the information he needs is freely available?

Free as Customer Expectation

Chris Anderson was one of the first to identify the way in which Free was becoming not just a business model, but an expectation. In his book *'Free: The Future of a Radical Price'*, Anderson refers to entertainment lawyer Jonathan Handel's six reasons why digital content will inevitably become free (comments are mine):

1. **The laws of supply and demand**: the supply of digital content has risen exponentially; conversely, demand has a limit because there's only so much stuff we can absorb. The price of content, therefore, has precipitously fallen.

2. **Loss of physical form**: once there's no physical artefact (newspaper, CD, film) we see it as intangible, and are therefore less willing to pay for it.

3. **Ease of access**: if we find it in a store we expect to pay for it, but if we instantly download it, we have neither time to think about the cost of producing it, nor do we have the inclination to pay for it.

4. **The shift to ad-supported content**: everyone knows Google makes its money (lots of it) out of advertising, so why can't content producers?

5. **Market forces in the technology industry**: There's more money in hardware than in software. Apple didn't expect to make much money when it launched iTunes – but it knew that we'd have to buy the iPods to play the music on. [5] This is a neat reversal of one of the earliest popular giveaways. Gillette gave away razors (hardware) so we'd buy the blades (software).

6. **Culture**: if you're under 30, then all you've known is that digital = free. It's a tough job for retailers to change that mindset.

---

[5] Recent performance suggest that iTunes is now turning a decent profit for Apple, enhancing still further Apple's profitability ratios.

This is why many young people don't seem to care about copyright – they believe information needs to be free in all senses of the word. When I worked in Liverpool in the late 1990s, there was an ambitious plan for the European Union to build a high-speed digital infrastructure for the city. I remember attending meetings where major IT companies were offering to almost give away their expertise and hardware, to provide the infrastructure – the servers and the pipes in the ground. I asked one of them how they were going to turn a profit out of this generosity. In a phrase which was just beginning to be heard at that time, I was told that 'content will be king'. The real money was to be made in the stuff that went through the pipes. They couldn't have been more wrong.

Free as User-Generated

My seventh point, (to add to Handel's six above), would therefore be one that the experts failed to see:

7. **Given the tools, we can produce too**: a participative, creative, citizenry may never have been envisioned, but it's here, so we'd better get used to it and to its willingness to produce freely.

In our journey to becoming *'prosumers'* (producers *and* consumers) it's interesting to see how long we clung on to the mantle of the expert. Even Jimmy Wales, founder of Wikipedia, believed that you'd have to pay experts to write articles that people would want to read. That was the logic behind Wikipedia's predecessor Nupedia. But academic experts don't do anything in a hurry, and Wales was left with a handful of articles after the first few months of commissioning.

Once the leap of faith in user-generated content was made, everything changed. Wikipedia went from a handful of articles in 2001, to its millionth article in just over 3 years. Since then, the growth of the blogosphere has also been exponential, and once Google bought YouTube in 2006, the afterburners were ignited.

The thing we all overlooked was this: people would gladly produce this content for free because the creation of it, plus a little audience recognition, was reward in itself. How did we have such a low opinion of ourselves that we couldn't acknowledge this possibility?

Which brings us back to Dan Brown. His *'Open Letter to Educators'* video is now being used as course content in masters of education programmes at a number of US universities. So someone's listening, Dan.

Free as a Business Model

Dan Brown's complaint that he was forced to buy books that he didn't really need highlights one of the last monopolies: academic publishing. How much longer a small cadre of publishers will be able to charge readers to access research that has already been funded through tax payers remains to be seen. I suspect that, at the least, they will be forced into adopting the financial model, which now dominates the internet. 'Freemium' offers basic services without charge, with higher-level use charged at a premium (though, in reality, because of negligible production costs, even 'premium' isn't particularly expensive).

The first major university to adopt Freemium was MIT, when they began to put all of their course materials online, for free. MIT Open CourseWare offers free videos, lecture notes, even past exams, in over 2,000 courses. One of their most popular courses is Physics 1: Classical Mechanics – yes, that's right, physics. The reason has less to do with the subject matter and more to do with the teacher.

Professor Walter Lewin recorded 36 lectures, which are some of the most engaging I've seen. The videos – covering everything from frictional forces to Heisenberg's uncertainty principle – were subsequently uploaded to YouTube, where some have had almost a million views. In keeping with the Global Learning Commons that MIT now maintains, students anywhere in the world can share questions and notes in the 'live study group'.

So, where's the 'premium' part of MIT's offer? Well, that lies in gaining accreditation. If you want those extras – like a degree – you're going to have to pay for them. That said, one suspects that MIT's motivation behind Open CourseWare is not to lure customers onto their paid-for programmes. Let's face it, they're not exactly short of applicants, are they?

Counter-intuitively, those who choose to make content free, in pursuit of the common good, often find that income streams look after themselves. In 2006, Salman Khan (a former graduate of MIT) quit his job as a hedge-fund trader to launch the Khan Academy, to offer online video tutorials in a range of subjects and at a range of levels (from beginner to post-graduate). With a mission to allow people to 'learn almost anything for free, when you want, at your own pace', Khan's academy has grown rapidly through a series of high-profile donations, from Bill Gates, Google and others. At the time of writing, the Khan Academy [6] had delivered 120 million 'lessons' – by the time you read this, there will have been many more.

As Anderson points out, free is rarely completely free – advertisers, cross-subsidisers, donors, all make free possible. But what we are seeing being played out in media boardrooms around the world are attempts to refashion business models, to see what the market will tolerate. When it comes to content,

---

[6] www.khanacademy.org

however, particularly digital content, we can learn from 'generation free': having grown up not paying for digital information, they will ensure that if isn't quite free it'll be considerably cheaper than it is right now.

So far, we have looked at free largely in monetary terms. But there are two further interpretations of Free that have become important values/actions, especially when trying to understand how learning can become more engaging.

Free to Fail

It's become a cliché in management literature that a vital ingredient in innovation is the freedom to fail. Most executives are aware that innovation can't really happen without the freedom to fail, but, as Vint Cerf, one of the 'founding fathers' of the internet, says: "There are many places where that freedom is not granted or at least it may not be explicit or very implicit, so the people with new ideas are not looked on with favor." [7]

Another challenge lies in responding to failure. Most often, freedom to fail is withdrawn because of simply not knowing how to turn failure into a positive and profitable learning experience. Many companies' failure response is the business equivalent of a social faux-pas at a party: pretend it never happened and change the focus of attention.

In our most innovative companies, however, a culture is shaped where failure embarrassment doesn't exist because it happens often, and learning what can be built upon, becomes the goal. At Google they call this 'fail fast and iterate'. Along with another of their mantras, 'everything's in beta', it's easy to see how they don't just talk about the freedom to fail – they walk it too. As Alan Noble, Google's Engineering Director, puts it, "If you have a work culture where bringing your mistakes to the

---

7 Interview with AOL Government 14th July 2011

table every week is a normal thing to do, it feels less like failing and more like learning".

It's estimated that in its twelve-year history, Google has publicly launched around 250 stand-alone products, of which 90 have been cancelled. Think about this stat for a minute: that's a 36 percent failure rate. How many companies would be comfortable with 36 percent failure? The answer of course, is one in which new ideas are flying thick and fast, learning is in the DNA, and where today's failure gets 'hacked' into tomorrow's success. Google Wave may have 'flopped', but the technology behind it was morphed into the much improved Google+.

Free as Entitlement

Successful businesses and schools alike are introducing the learner's 'right-to-roam': the freedom to learn where your interests and passions lead you. 3M were probably the first company to offer a 15 percent free-time entitlement, where employees could work on their own passions and projects. Others are now taking working freedoms still further. Electronics retail giant, Best Buy, was one of the first companies to offer their office staff the flexibility to come and go as they pleased. So long as their personal targets were met, Best Buy didn't care how long, or where, they worked.

The results were startling: productivity and employee engagement and retention rose sharply. The two employees, Cali Ressler and Jodi Thompson, credited with successfully implementing what is now known as a 'Results Only Work Environment' (ROWE) now advise other companies looking to introduce ROWE. Fashion retailer, Gap Outlet, piloted a programme in 2008 that allowed employees to show up when they needed to, and leave for home when they wanted to. Facing a high degree of scepticism, the introduction of ROWE has had dramatic results: in a single year, productivity rose 21 percent; employee engagement rose by 19 percent, and work/life balance scores were up 10 percent.

Once again, education struggles with the concept of learners having freedom to follow their passions. Just as Gap's managers were afraid that handing over the responsibility for 'being there' to staff would result in mass indolence, schools and universities fret that giving more freedoms and responsibilities to learners will result in empty classrooms, missed targets and the curriculum not being 'covered'.

Yet, one of the longest-established radical experiments in learner freedoms, Summerhill School, founded by A. S. Neill in 1921, has always given learners the choice of what they learn, or indeed whether to attend classes or not. Received wisdom would predict that without strict discipline and highly-structured learning programmes, young children would behave 'irresponsibly'. The school's exam results, however, are better than average, and the English government's schools inspectorate in 2011 deemed Summerhill 'good with many outstanding features'.

The great American philosopher, John Dewey, once said, "Schools should teach everything that anyone is interested in learning". You've got to admit, it's hard to argue against that as a mission statement.

*****

All of the above interpretations of Free have game-changing significance for learning, everywhere it happens. They all have strong elements of counter-intuition, which probably explains why so few leaders make the leap of faith needed to make them work. But society is making inexorable shifts in changing how, what and where we learn.

They're being driven by some basic rights in accessing knowledge, in employee and learner entitlements and in our frustration with the erosion of our autonomy. If we want our companies and schools to thrive in the next decade we need to incorporate them into our learning environments.

Trust

The previous three values and actions all rely, for their impact, upon the fourth: Trust.

Most of the examples listed here would be doomed to failure if it weren't for Trust. The crowd being sourced by Proctor & Gamble, Nokia, and others has to trust that the provenance of its ideas will be respected. Tony Hsieh has to trust that Zappos' customers will see their transparency as a desire to form an honest relationship with them, not a sign of incompetence. And we all have to trust Google to handle the mass of data they hold on us, responsibly. Teachers have to trust that their students, given more freedom and more responsibility, will exceed their expectations (they nearly always do).

In Ourselves We Trust

In recent years, although we've lost trust in many of our major pillars of contemporary life – banks, media, politicians and the police – we've rediscovered our trust in each other. Now, I don't want to be naive about this: I know there are scammers, spammers, fraudsters and hoaxers to be found all over the internet. But the remarkable thing is how services that rely on user trust have gained in popularity over the past 10 years.

If memory allows, try to recall the first time you won an eBay auction. Did you doubt that you would ever receive the item, after paying for it? I know that I did. Now, however, we buy and sell without a second thought, and with some justification, since less than one percent of eBay purchases result in fraud.

Even more remarkable is the growth of a site like Couchsurfing.com where hosts in a city offer free accommodation to visitors. Despite being conditioned by a media which, a decade ago, would have classed such an act as 'asking for trouble', there has been a growing acceptance that offering your couch to a foreign guest isn't just an act of kindness – the host also benefits from the cultural insights gained.

Couchsurfing isn't a 'something for something' service – only around 12 percent of friendships are reciprocated – but there is a generalised reciprocity, paying acts of generosity forward. In less than seven years Couchsurfing has built a membership of over 3 million people around the world, with abuse of trust incidence microscopically low.

The trust we place in such interactions works because of the service providers' 'reputation system'. eBay buyers and sellers understand the importance of positive feedback (fewer than five percent of auctions attract negative feedback), and because there are risks to personal safety, Couchsurfing has a set of identity verifications, friendship ratings and 'vouch for' mechanisms, in addition to feedback ratings. These words are being written in Australia, where I am swapping my house in the UK with people I have never met. The reciprocity and reputation systems give me confidence that the house will be as I left it upon my return. (Update: It wasn't – it was better.)

The rise of reputation-based social sites confirms what we knew all along – that we want people to think well of us, and that we want to trust our fellow citizens – it's simply that, up until now, we never had the tools to show what we could do for each other, given the chance. A spirit that was previously only seen between neighbours now spans the globe.

Trust in Business

Whilst valuing trust may seem like a natural fit for the social space, it has always been a harder sell in the corporate world. Ron Shaich had built the Panera Bread Company into one of the biggest bakery brands in America, but was curious to see if trust made business, as well as social, sense. In May 2010 he opened the Panera Cares Community Cafe in Colorado. There are no prices in the cafe, and no cash registers. People put what they can afford into a donations box, (thus preserving everyone's dignity) and if they can't afford anything they volunteer an hour or so of their time.

As a social experiment, it worked. On average, 20 percent of people pay more than the normal selling price, because they know they are supporting the 20 percent who pay a little less. And because running costs are low, thanks to the volunteers, the cafe is thriving. Shaich's plan is to open four more community cafes per year, on a not-for-profit basis (but hopefully not-for-loss either).

The importance of trust in how corporations create an effective working environment could not be more important, according to the people who judge it. The Great Place To Work Institute has 25 years of research which shows, year-on-year, that when employees are asked 'what's the most important reason for staying here?' it isn't the subsidised lunches, or other perks: it's trust. Moreover, Great Place to Work have noted a direct correlation between the level to which employees feel trusted by their bosses, and the profit made by the company.

When Trust Goes Missing

Trust is often linked to accountability through the process of target setting in both private and public sectors. In this context, we are told that accountability helps reinforce trust. I don't believe this has ever been the case. Instead, accountability is usually what's left after trust has been removed. The visionary management consultant, W.E. Deming, once described attempts to make everyone accountable as 'ridiculous', claiming that 'whenever there is fear, you will get wrong figures'.

The erosion of trust in public school systems has had catastrophic consequences, and will take decades to put right. As we've seen, attempts to make schools 'more accountable' for their test scores leave teachers torn between what psychologist Barry Schwartz calls 'doing the right thing and doing the required thing'. The right thing is to teach students through personalised, flexible methods, according to their needs, interests and aspirations; the required thing is to 'turnaround' test scores, by 'teaching to the test' or, worse, 'gaming' the system.

Successive US federal administrations have sought to improve school standards through high accountability. The pressure this puts upon schools at risk of closure and teachers – with test scores linked to pay rates – is intense. During 2011/12 a series of allegations emerged of inner-city schools in New York, Washington DC, Atlanta and Philadelphia 'cheating' on student test scores in order to hit accountability targets. Undoubtedly a case of fear producing wrong figures.

The result of doing the required thing, above the right thing, is what Schwartz describes as a 'de-moral-ised' profession. The double tragedy is that, in addition to the pressure put on teachers – 50 percent of new teachers in the US leave the profession within their first five years – there's growing evidence that the over-reliance on standardised testing fails to improve academic learning anyway.

The US National Research Council's Committee on Incentives and Test-Based Accountability recently produced a damning report showing that increasing student performance on high stakes tests not only did not increase student achievement in other measures of academic ability, but also had a detrimental effect on graduation rates. Other incentives, including linking teacher pay to exam results, or paying students to pass exams produced similarly disappointing results.[8]

Contrast this culture of distrust, deception and demoralisation with the Finnish schools system. For over a decade, Finland has consistently topped the OECD's international comparisons on students' achievements in reading, writing, maths and sciences. Politicians and education experts have speculated on the reasons behind Finland's success.

Pasi Sahlberg, Director of Finland's Centre for International Mobility, is in no doubt. He defines the 'new culture', which transformed the relationship between government and schools in the 1990s, in this way: "Basic to this new culture is the cultivation of trust between education authorities and schools. Such trust as we then witnessed made reform not only sustainable, but also owned by teachers." [9]

It seems that we could learn a lot about trust from Nordic educators. In 2009 students in Danish schools were allowed to access the internet during final examinations. They could use any sites, but were not allowed to message or email each other. The Danish government argued, with devastating logic that if the internet is so much a part of daily life, it should be included in classrooms and exams. One of the teachers leading the pilot was asked by the BBC what precautions were put in place to prevent cheating. "The main precaution", she replied, "is that we trust them." You can't say fairer than that, can you?

*****

---

[8] Hoult, M. and Elliott, S. *'Incentives and Test-based Accountability in Education'* (2011) National Research Council
[9] Sahlberg, P. *'Finnish Lessons: What Can The World Learn From Educational Change in Finland?'* (2012) Teachers College Press

The Inevitability of SOFT

I've argued here that the four values and actions of Share, Open, Free and Trust are reshaping how we socially interact with one another. Since, with sufficient eyeballs and sufficient clicks, we can inevitably get access to information that's being hidden from us, we want to be treated like grown-ups.

We want to take more control of our lives, so we harness the wisdom of crowds, and the power of social media, to make all kinds of decisions, which used to be the domain of 'experts' in the past. Because we have so much more control of our social lives, we want to have more say in the way we work, and we'll trade that freedom for higher salaries in choosing whom we work for. We want that freedom and self-direction in how we learn too, or we'll vote with our feet, as Dan Brown did. We want people to think well of us, so we engage in acts of generosity, which require degrees of trust and risk, but increase our social reputation.

We do all of these, not because we're somehow different people in the 21st century, but because we now have the tools and networks to be able to do so. We act SOFT, because we can.

Since these values and actions have become so prevalent in the social space, our smarter businesses and our smarter schools, colleges and education systems are beginning to put them at the core of their mission, and of their strategies. Those that are ahead of the curve, like Google and Zappos, are finding that SOFT is not just good for customer and employee relations, it's good for turnover, too. Those that are dragging their heels, like the UK and US education authorities, are not only struggling with disengaged and demoralised staff, they are seeing no increase in performance, despite a whole heap of greater accountability.

It's simply inevitable that, having helped shape how we now live, and work, these values will become central to how we learn. Embedding SOFT values into innovative learning environments is not without its dangers. Giving employees and learners greater freedom demands greater responsibility. Being transparent may provide disgruntled employees with the means to act maliciously. But we have to learn how to adapt, and we have to adapt how we learn. As W.E. Deming once said 'Learning isn't compulsory...neither is survival'.

Chapter Four

The Global Learning Commons –
the site of the Open Revolution

There is something that connects the most innovative and successful companies, educational institutions and social collectives. Despite holding very different visions and values, they share many of the same characteristics in the way they learn. They manage to combine culture, structure, ambience and space to create exceptional learning environments.

I call it the Global Learning Commons, and it's the place where 'open' can be seen at its dynamic best. It connects the local to the global, the private to the public, and the formal to the social. It also blurs the boundaries between social strata, the amateur and the professional, work and play.

It can justifiably be called a commons because, like the 'common lands' of the Middle Ages, there is a simple concept of 'all that we share' at the heart of it. Up until the 17th century, the right of English 'commoners' to graze livestock, build dwellings, and fish on manorial property in Britain worked to almost everyone's satisfaction. Land was used efficiently, people shared what was tended, and the landowner was grateful that his domain was well maintained.

Sadly, over the following three centuries, a succession of parliamentary acts, triggered by landowner greed, dramatically reduced communal access and rights of way. The so-called 'enclosure movement' insidiously fenced off lands in the name of greater efficiency/profit, and a way of life had begun to erode.

An historical metaphor also seems appropriate because, thanks to digital technologies, we are starting to see some ancient values and principles being revived in how we co-exist socially. There is, however, another reason for using the metaphor of the commons: the battle for the stewardship of public resources is as hotly contested today as it was in medieval Britain. The history of land use has been characterised as a struggle between those who believed in the 'common good' – taking only what was needed and contributing their labour and resources without the guarantee of a return – and those who believed in enclosing land, and attributing ownership of it so as to maximise production, and profit.

The enclosure movement effectively brought market forces into agriculture. But for every person who saw this as the inevitable march of progress, there were others who, even in the 17th century, were advocating reclamation. The Diggers, for example, were a group of protesters who dug up and cultivated common land, in an effort to reclaim land grabs that had been legislated by the ruling classes. In many ways, the Occupy protesters are little more than the latest manifestation of the Diggers.

The Learning Commons in the 21st Century

The erosion of common resources happens by stealth. There is, however, increasing interest in reclaiming the concept of the commons through a current swathe of social movements. When I first used the term, Global Learning Commons, I felt sure that there would already be a well-formed set of arguments for seeing learning as a common resource. 'On The Commons', the most visible advocacy group for reclaiming common resources, boasts an impressive list of areas in which it's active:

information, economy, environment, food, culture, politics, health, science.

Until very recently, however, education has been conspicuous by its absence. Perhaps the best known campaigners for bringing the commons principles to learning has been the Creative Commons movement. Founded in 2001 by Harvard Law Professor Lawrence Lessig, Creative Commons has argued that copyright laws have become overly-restrictive, curtailing creativity and the creation of a 'public domain' of works. They have persuaded many writers and artists (and latterly educators) to license their work for re-use in non-commercial contexts.

Creative Commons has supported the 'Open Educational Resources' coalition, and an impressive list of educational institutions, including the Khan Academy and MIT, are committed to making their materials free to learners and open to adaption by teachers.

What I mean by the Global Learning Commons, however, goes beyond the licensing of rights, important though they are, or making resources free. It encompasses the 'ecology' of learning: the relationships we have with each other; the creation of an hospitable habitat for learning; how we cultivate the evolution of learning in communal, social environments, to transfer it successfully to others, establishing a set of commonly-agreed principles which will make learning inclusive and innovative.

As I described earlier, 'open' isn't some far-distant aspiration – it's already happening, it's just not evenly distributed. Of the three spaces where learning happens – in work, in education and in society – we are witnessing the most radical change in the way we learn outside our formal institutions. Why? Because outside of work, school or college, we, the learners, can be in charge, it is 'free' time. In the social (and increasingly virtual) spaces, learning isn't done *to* us, it's done *by* us. We have no compulsory training courses to attend, no national curriculum we're forced to follow.

So, because we are learning, simply for the love of it, we create a learning commons. And because the technology allows us to, we've made it global. With notable exceptions (and we'll look at them in detail later) most of the organised learning that occurs in corporations and in schools has been distorted by enclosures, separating learning into 'subjects' and learners into units of production.

It's the equivalent of erecting fences on 17th-century common land in order to make farming more efficient. Economically, it may have been effective (although some would dispute that), but the sense of common good was lost. Similarly, enclosing learning may have efficiently processed learners and served employers needs during an industrial era, but it's now an anachronism. Allow me to give a personal illustration by way of example.

Having been led to believe that the misery I endured at school was a thing of the past, my own introduction to work-based learning, came as something of a shock to the system. I began my working life as a junior clerk in a department of the UK civil service. Admittedly, the idea of being a government bureaucrat didn't set my pulse racing but when you were 17 in 1970s north-east England you basically had three choices: the shipyards, the mines or the office. It was the lesser of three evils. But nothing could have done a better job of deadening my soul than my induction course.

A group of us sat in a large hall. On each desk was placed a ledger that was at least six inches thick. We were told this was 'the Bible' – a manual that gave instructions for every possible eventuality we would meet in our clerical duties. A trainer instructed us to open it at page one, and, for the next 3 weeks, we proceeded to work our soulless way through it. It was a scene so Dickensian that if Bob Cratchit, from A Christmas Carol, had told us to 'buy another coal-scuttle before you dot another i', none of us would have looked up.

I'm not suggesting that we should have brainstormed a Post-It Note session on the best way to administer maternity benefit claims, but it was enough to make me realise that this was not a work culture in which I would thrive. I lasted a year before telling my line-manager that I was going to become a professional musician, to which he responded (and I promise you he actually said this to my 17-year-old self): "But what about your pension?"

Of course, I'm sure the Department of Work and Pensions is a far more creative place to work in nowadays, and it needs to be. The pace of societal change is outstripping the slow evolution of learning, so we need some new ideas in formal learning if we're to avoid irrelevance.

The learning, taking place in the global commons is innovative, constantly adapting to new contexts and, for those schools, universities and businesses that adopt its characteristics, it's proving to be measurably transformative. In the chapters that follow, I'll share some great examples of learning in each of the three spaces, but first I should identify the characteristics and principles that shape the Global Learning Commons.

Participation, Passion, and Purpose in the Global Learning Commons

Any commons is essentially a shared resource, which works through carefully balancing rights and responsibilities. As it is with air, or water, so it should be with learning. Your right of access to the knowledge and skills of others is balanced with a responsibility to share what you can offer. So, the first characteristic of the Global Learning Commons is **participation**.

The most innovative learning spaces are open, reciprocal and participatory – learning doesn't really work as a spectator sport, as any disengaged school kid will confirm. Hierarchy and status get in the way of collaborative learning, and the learning commons should have low, or no, entry barriers. Diversity is good – innovative learning environments can't operate as knowledge country clubs, for, as author James Surowiecki demonstrated, the wisdom of crowds is dependent upon diversity, and multiple perspectives.[1]

Now you may be thinking that democratic participation, through rights and responsibilities, is a recipe for confusion, if not chaos. If you are, let me tell you about Valve, the company behind some of the world's bestselling video games, including Half-Life, Portal and Counter-Strike. Had I encountered their staff manual when I was 17, I might never have become a musician. It is posted publicly and I'd urge you to download it.[2] It's as confoundingly counter-intuitive as it is humorous, telling newly-arrived staff that Valve is 'flat':

> "It's our shorthand way of saying that we don't have any management, and nobody "reports to" anybody else. We do have a founder/president, but even he isn't your manager. This company is yours to steer—toward opportunities and away from risks. You have the power to green-light projects. You have the power to ship products... If you're thinking to yourself, "Wow, that sounds like a lot of responsibility," you're right... Since Valve is flat, people don't join projects because they're told to. Instead, you'll decide what to work on after asking

---

[1] Surowiecki, J. (2004) The Wisdom of Crowds, Doubleday

[2] www.newcdn.flamehaus.com/Valve_Handbook_LowRes.pdf

yourself the right questions. Employees vote on projects with their feet (or desk wheels). Strong projects are ones in which people can see demonstrated value; they staff up easily. This means there are any number of internal recruiting efforts constantly under way."

The clue to Valve's success, and the glue which binds individual motives into corporate coherence, lies in its learning environment:

"...you're now surrounded by a multidisciplinary group of experts in all kinds of fields—creative, legal, financial, even psychological. Many of these people are probably sitting in the same room as you every day, so the opportunities for learning are huge. Take advantage of this fact whenever possible: the more you can learn about the mechanics, vocabulary, and analysis within other disciplines, the more valuable you become."

Depending upon your personality, and ability to work without supervision, this could seem like work heaven, or hell. But, you can't knock its achievements. Founded in 1996 with no venture capital, 16 years later, Valve, a non-hierarchical, apparently anarchic, certainly autonomous, group of more than 300 employees without a boss, was worth $3 billion.

Learning commons are also characterised by the second characteristic: **passion**. Great learning environments aren't afraid of passion, because of its key role in motivation. Being passionate in formal learning situations is so unexpected that it's frequently confused with eccentricity.

Our norms in the workplace and in school have come to faintly disapprove of such behaviour. Yet one only has to look at examples of great teaching and learning lauded on social media, to see that passion is exactly what we want to see.

The aforementioned Walter Lewin (emeritus professor at MIT college) is possibly the most popular professor on YouTube. In most senses, his approach is precisely what disengaged students complain about – chalk and talk, with little opportunity for student discussion.

But Prof. Lewin has three great skills: an ability to make complex ideas graspable; a flair for theatrical demonstrations (the clip of his chin just millimetres away from a wildly oscillating wrecking ball has become the stuff of legend), and great passion. The title of his last book, 'For The Love Of Physics', says it all.

As brilliant as he is, Lewin is something of an exception, and the covert filming of classroom life on mobile phones now offers us a glimpse of what goes on in our schools. Ordinarily, it's the dumb or the frivolous that gets shared. But, occasionally, an uploaded video resonates because it demonstrates how lacking in passion formal learning, at its worst, can be.

In May 2013 a student in Duncanville High School in Dallas, Texas, uploaded to YouTube footage of a fellow student, Jeff Bliss, being ejected from class. In a mere 90 seconds, Bliss offers a crushing indictment of passionless teaching, delivered passionately. Conversely, his teacher's side of the discussion includes monotone instructions to *"quit bitching"*, *"you're wasting my time"*, *"just get out of my class"*. For his part, Jeff Bliss[3], gets to the heart of the problem:

"If you could just get up and teach 'em, instead of handing them a frickin' packet. There's kids in here who don't learn like that. They need to learn face-to-face... you want kids

---

[3] www.youtube.com/watch?v=3bYv2AKPZOk

to get excited for this, you gotta come in here and make 'em excited. If you want a kid to change and start doing better, you gotta touch his frickin' heart."

His teacher listed her professional goal on her LinkedIn profile thus: 'To bring quality content and experiences to enrich the lives of my students in the classroom and beyond'. I've no doubt that she was sincere in this aspiration. But her modus operandi, if this incident was anything to go by, was to dish out packets of notes and worksheets to students. Any teacher can have a bad day but what is shocking about the clip, viewed by millions, and the follow-up comments, and media discussion, is how routinely our young people experience such dispassionate teaching.

Is it the educational system that grinds the enthusiasm out of our teachers? Perhaps teachers now expect compliance, and therefore can't cope if they see their students passionate about their learning? I once watched a teacher eject a student for being too excited about the task in hand. When I asked why he'd done so, he said that 'If I allow one to get excited, they'll all think it's OK, and then it would be chaos!' Gosh, a classroom full of excited learners – we can't have that, can we?

But it isn't just in school where we have issues with passion. The office staff training sessions have become such a rich source of parody (witness 'The Office' sitcom staff training episode) that they point to a deep truth: the formal learning environment doesn't cope very well with either passionate educators or learners. Of course, there are millions of committed, passionate teachers out there in our classrooms – we just find it difficult to value them.

Passion is also a key factor in engagement. The notion of engagement, and disengagement, in learning is so important that I have given it a section of its own, coming up shortly. One final comment on passion: one of the remarkable changes that going 'open' has brought about, is to simultaneously shrink the world (in terms of distance of communication) whilst expanding its complexity. It's never been easier to tap into other people's passions. We can Skype experts from around the world to help us solve problems on the street where we live. A learning commons allows us to think, and act, locally and globally, about things that really matter to us.

The final Global Learning Commons characteristic is **purpose**. It's surprising how often formalised learning lacks clear purpose: staff training operating 'because we've always done it like this'; students covering historical events 'because it's on the test'; the failure of governments to articulate the purpose of compulsory schooling. In the GLC, purpose is two-fold: independence (to allow people to do things for themselves, and interdependence (to enable groups to collaborate and learn from each other).

The African farmer we met in Chapter Two, who discovers the solution to ants destroying his potato crop recognises the interdependence of his neighbours, so pins the wood-ash treatment to the village noticeboard. In part this is out of self-interest – if his neighbours don't also treat their crops the ants could return to his crop – but it is mainly through an implicit reciprocity. By sharing what he has learned, it is more likely that others will do the same and that he will benefit in the future.

The internet, itself a prime example of a Global Learning Commons, is filled with like-minded groups, seeking combinations of self-sufficiency and self-determination. Human beings have always had these desires, but now they have the means. So, the act of learning itself becomes more purposeful, not simply acquiring knowledge, but putting it to good use.

Of course, not all groups have benevolent intent, and their existence is often used as a reason to erect fences around the worldwide web. But, in the so-called 'battle for the internet', the fact that millions, perhaps billions, of people are collaboratively learning, in order to improve lives, is a pretty powerful argument for keeping it 'open'.

The Industrial and The Horticultural

In the pressure-filled world inhabited by politicians and CEOs, their desire to see learning as a quasi-mechanical process is understandable. They want to see predictable outputs from a replicable input: teaching. Predictability is what we'd all like to see. Talent managers and human resources want to be able to predict the impact of company training courses.

Publicly, we continue to describe learning as an industrial process, created by state education systems, which needed to prepare workers for the factory and the production line. Successive strategies have inevitably tried to crank the levers of teaching to increase learning outputs, variably known as examination results, or increased productivity/profits.

From the late 20th century onwards, the language of learning has become disconcertingly industrialised. Learning isn't nurtured – it's 'delivered'. Effective learning is defined as linear (like a production line) and sequential. If output falls, schools and colleges are made accountable, and the process of improvement has to be accelerated.

The trouble is, nothing about the industrial metaphor of learning is appropriate for the post-industrial age we're living in. Apart from a small number of innovative companies, schools and colleges, we seem unable to rethink learning for the knowledge age. In part, this is because much of what is said about the process of education avoids any reference to how people actually learn.

The Global Learning Commons recognises that a leader's responsibility is to create the fertile conditions that support learners in their growth, but to accept that, however frustrating it might be for those who are accountable for results, learning is ultimately an act of self-determination.

How different would employee training programmes and school improvement strategies look if we incorporated some of the following Learning Commons' principles:

1. No one can be 'made' to learn anything: for knowledge and understanding to stick, we have to have learner intent. The quality of one's learning is directly related to our desire to learn. This is why progress made in learning socially, voluntarily, is invariably far greater than in the formal, compulsory context.

2. We can't motivate learners to learn: many teachers believe it's their job to motivate their students. It's not. They can only truly motivate themselves. But a great teacher helps learners see the relevance which drives self-motivation – why learning something will make a difference in their lives.

3. Engagement precedes learning: learning becomes an uphill struggle without deep absorption in a task, (what the psychologist Mihaly Csikszentmihalyi calls being 'in the flow' – unaware of time passing). Learning without engagement is likely to be superficial, temporary. Engaged learning has depth and 'stickiness'.

4. When it comes to learning, informal beats formal: the organisation learning expert, Jay Cross, asserts that between 70 and 90 percent of learning in organisations is informally acquired. When surveyed, there appears to be a consensus among learning and development officers of a 70:20:10 learning ratio at play: 70 percent of learning is gained on the job, through experience; 20 percent is

gained through coaching or mentoring; 10 percent is through formal, structured courses. Cross further claims that formal learning is the least efficient: 'study after study has shown that only about 15 percent of what's learned in a formal setting is ever actually applied on the job'. [4]Similar surveys conducted with young students favour informal learning. When asked 'How do you prefer to learn?' Most students choose 'from friends/family' first, followed by 'the internet', followed by 'my teacher'.

5. Recalling information is not the same as knowing: industrial teaching strategies favour retention and recollection, and formulaic solutions to problems, rather than higher-order or critical-thinking skills. I can study the actions of a swimmer, recall the necessary coordination of movements, so that I could be said to know 'about' swimming. But I still don't know 'how' to swim. That requires repeated application of such knowledge, until some level of aquatic mastery (i.e. not sinking) is acquired. Schools are under pressure to get students to 'know about' a large amount of content, so that it can be successfully regurgitated in an examination hall. But students subsequently progressing to university often fail to cope with the higher-order skills demanded there.

6. An individual's capacity to learn is constantly changing, and is affected by a wide range of personal self-perceptions: Stanford Professor Carol Dweck, in her book 'Mindset', powerfully argues that a learner with a fixed mindset, believing their intelligence is limited, and a

---

4 Xyleme Voices Podcast Interview with Harold Jarche, Charles Jennings, Jay Cross, Clark Quinn www.xyleme.com/podcasts/archives/16

product of brains and talent, rather than effort, will learn less well than a learner with a growth mindset who recognises their own potential, and capacity for improvement. How we think we learn – in the jargon, our 'meta-cognitive' capacity to know ourselves as learners – has a crucial bearing upon how we actually learn.

If you've ever wondered why you can't remember much of what you learned in schools just a couple of years after leaving, it's probably because most of the above list was ignored while teaching you. The process of learning is an intensely personal one and, as much as we'd like to believe that there was a simple 'input-output' equation, there isn't.

There's one further side-effect of the industrialisation of learning: it invariably becomes a corporate activity, carried out for personal, or corporate, profit or gain. So, teachers in schools are now judged solely by their ability to improve test scores. Learning and development managers in corporations are beset by the need to prove that their learning programmes positively impact upon 'the bottom line'.

The industrial model of learning – be it in the college or the corporation – not only creates enclosures, it promotes isolation and risk-aversion. The Global Learning Commons matters because it restores learning to its original function: as a public act, collaboratively undertaken for civic empowerment and improvement.

*****

I'm aware that advocating participation, passion and purpose is all very well, but it will cut no ice with those hardened by the school of 'deliverology' unless it can be proven to be more effective, and more efficient. Examples of great learning commons in the formal sphere may still be in the minority, but they are growing, and they are highly successful. In the next few chapters, we will see how creating a social learning environment can make a company a powerhouse of invention, how giving away your intellectual assets can restore a failing company to its former greatness and how schools can propel college and employment statistics off the charts by encouraging students to co-design their learning.

Chapter Five

Getting Engaged

During the time that I've been writing this book, a sobering realisation, at least in Europe and North America, has taken hold. Recovery from the financial meltdown of 2008 is going to take decades, not years. So, one inevitable consequence of adjusting to the new economic reality is that, if we're not able to tempt employees with high salaries, company bosses will be under even more pressure to make work a more fulfilling and satisfying place to be.

And here, at last, there's some good news: we've set a very low bar. Levels of employee engagement and employee autonomy couldn't be much lower if we were all working in Solzhenitsyn's Gulag Archipelago.

Living, as we are, through an age of corporate austerity, it might seem like bad timing to be advocating employee engagement. CEOs could be forgiven for thinking that employee engagement comes a poor second behind financial survival. Making employees more productive might seem like a smarter move than keeping them engaged. A stream of studies in recent years, however, has demonstrated an irrefutable link between employee engagement, innovation and profitability. Too often CEOs see engagement as not contributing to the bottom-line. Nothing could be further from the truth. Some of the most profitable and innovative companies in the world also have the most engaged employees.

The logic chain goes like this: to survive in a cut-throat market, businesses need innovation to be a core function; innovation demands creativity; creativity comes out of curiosity (and learning); engagement is a necessary precursor to both. As Professor Julian Birkinshaw of the London Business School argues, "employee engagement is the sine qua non of innovation. In my experience ... you cannot foster true innovation without engaged employees."[1]

The estimated cost in lost productivity of employee disengagement is $300bn per year *in the US alone.*[2] It's perhaps understandable that, having suffered one of the deepest and longest-lasting economic recessions in living memory, most companies in the West understandably place employee engagement a long way behind survival in their strategic priorities. But losing $300bn a year shows the financial cost of overlooking engagement.

The largest study in recent years – The Towers Perrin Global Workforce Study – surveyed over half a million employees from 50 companies around the world. It reported a 52 percent gap in improved operating income between companies with high and low employee engagement scores. Similarly, a Gallup report in 2007 asked workers if their job brought out their most creative ideas: 59 percent of engaged employees replied positively, while only three percent of disengaged employees did so. That's why engagement matters.

Harvard Business Professor, Teresa Amabile, has studied what makes the difference between successful and unsuccessful companies. Her conclusion? Forget incentive schemes, and

---

[1] Quoted in *Engaging for Success: enhancing performance through Employee Engagement* 2009 Dept. for Business, Innovation and Skills
[2] Employee Engagement Overview, 2010, Gallup

concentrate on the 'inner work life' of employees: their emotions, perceptions and intrinsic motivations. Amabile claims inner work life is a key element of employee engagement, which in turn drives performance, and she will happily quote from other studies highlighting the links between job satisfaction and company performance.[3]

If these correlation-ships seem obvious (and they should) you have to wonder why so few company executives 'get it'. How else to explain the appallingly low rates of employee engagement? Surveys consistently estimate workers defined as not engaged, or disengaged at 60 percent, or higher. Gallup's 2011 survey presented a worsening picture, with grave implications for worker morale:

"The overall results indicate that 11 percent of workers worldwide are engaged. In other words, about one in nine employees worldwide is emotionally connected to their workplaces and feels he or she has the resources and support they need to succeed. The majority of workers, 62%, are not engaged – that is, emotionally detached and likely to be doing little more than is necessary to keep their jobs. And 27 percent are actively disengaged, indicating they view their workplaces negatively and are liable to spread that negativity to others." [4]

Engagement has an impact in almost every aspect of work: employee well-being (disengaged employees take almost three times the number of sickness days off, compared to engaged workers); company loyalty (engaged employees are 87 percent less likely to leave their job), and customer relations (a 53

[3] Teresa Amabile Google Talk 'The Progress Principle' 15th August 2011

[4] *The State of The Global Workplace: A Worldwide Study of Employee Engagement and Well-Being* (2011) Gallup Consulting

percent gap in understanding customer needs, between the engaged and disengaged employee).

Permission To Think

Employee engagement has fallen consistently in recent decades, and the underlying causes are varied. Loss of autonomy is clearly one. In 1986, 72 percent of professionals felt they had a 'great deal' of independence doing their jobs. By 2006, that number had fallen to 38 percent.

A shift to employees working from a script has become all too apparent in some jobs. We've all experienced the frustration that often comes when we have to call for an insurance quote, or technical support, and are put through to a scripted conversation with someone in a call centre. Increasingly, however, we see this loss of autonomy in more senior roles. It used to be that a visit to your local general practitioner sparked a doctor-to-patient discussion. Now, (if my personal experience is typical) it's doctor-to-computer.

During the writing of this chapter, I visited my doctor to ask for some blood tests, as I was struggling to shake off a virus. In order to simply attach a label to my blood going off to the test lab, she had to follow a screen-by-screen set of questions: had I been abroad recently? (if yes to 'Far East', test for avian flu); unusual bowel motions? (test for Coeliac Disease). It was faintly comical to see her trying to request a test for Clostridium Difficile, only to be told that the computer said 'no'.

As the lab labels spewed out of her printer she was instructed to 'affix label A to red vial', and so on... OK, we know that mistakes happen, but seeing seven years of training and 20-years' professional practice reduced to a series of tick boxes must be quite dispiriting.

According to the Guardian's Aditya Chakrabortty this loss of autonomy for professional white-collar workers is only going to get worse in the near future due to the impact of technology and knowledge process outsourcing. Citing the academic I quoted in Chapter One, Phillip Brown, Chakrabortty paints a depressing picture:

> "If you're a bank manager you have far fewer individual powers than your predecessor would have had in the 80s. And if you're a teller, it's standard practice to work from a script... a high-up banker who used to be in charge of lending decisions (finds) his expertise has now been supplanted by a credit controller, described as "a software package that automatically assesses a loan application according to specific criteria" Brown and his colleagues talk about a future workforce in which only 10-15% will have "permission to think." The rest of us will merely carry out their decisions...think call centres rather than groovy offices and you're most of the way there."

If loss of autonomy is a factor in the erosion of engagement, loss of trust is another. As we saw in Chapter Three, productivity inevitably rises when workers feel secure and happy. Yet a 2010 survey found that 53 percent of workers felt that their boss didn't treat them as a professional equal, with 37 percent saying their boss had 'thrown them under the bus' to save themselves.[5]

Curiously, when employee engagement surveys are conducted, an employee's attitude to learning and development doesn't seem to be a factor – precisely because no one ever asks them about it.

Items on engagement surveys frequently highlight clarity of job purpose, employer trust, feedback and support from

---

[5] *The 2010 Bass Day Survey*, conducted by Monster on behalf of Spherion Staffing

supervisors, perceptions of organisational values, quality of working relationships, but almost never the extent to which an employee feels they are learning and personally developing. As we shall see, student engagement isn't exactly a cause for celebration either, but almost all student engagement surveys at least recognise the importance of learning.

What lies beneath the absence of learning as a factor in employee engagement? Could it be that so much learning in the workplace is tacit – acquired informally through observation and osmosis – that we simply don't see it, and therefore under-value it? Are formal opportunities, provided through classroom-based training and almost universally viewed as 'boring', giving the role of learning at work a bad name? Or do employers simply see an employee's knowledge and skills as something to be mined, not replenished?

Whatever the reasons, when we look at successful companies who have created innovative learning environments, it's clear that the learning context is both a powerful performance motivator and a significant factor in holding on to good staff. Employers ignore the connection between learning and engagement at their peril.

What Did You Do In School Today?

Engagement in formal education mirrors engagement in the workplace. Student engagement – or rather, the lack of it – in schools and colleges, is perhaps the number one cause for concern among educators. The statistics are distressing:

- 98 percent of US students feel bored at school at least some of the time; two-thirds feel bored every day; 17 percent say they are bored *every* lesson. [6]

---

[6] *Charting the Path from Engagement to Achievement: A report on the 2009 High School Survey of Student Engagement* (2009) Indiana University

- 10 percent of English students claim to 'hate' school. [7]

- Estimates of English 14 to 16-year-olds defining themselves as 'disengaged' vary from 20-33 percent. These students are predominantly white, male, and from disadvantaged backgrounds, and are most likely to truant.[8]

- Engagement decreases progressively – In Canada 82 percent of Grade 5 students are intellectually engaged in school. By grade 11 that number has halved. Only 31 percent of students are interested in and motivated to learn, in Canadian. [9]

- One in four American high school students drop out of school each year. 80 percent of US students don't see how school contributes to their learning, and 60 percent don't list learning as the reason they go to school.[10]

As depressing as these stats may be, I personally find the values and aspirations that lie behind the statistics to be more worrying. I would be willing to bet that a parent, being confronted with these figures, is more than likely to respond with a 'Yes, and?'

As someone who has been passionate about getting students more engaged in their learning, I'm never less than surprised at adult expectations – it's as if we no longer expect students to be engaged in school, just so long as they're achieving and keeping out of trouble.

In attempting to rationalise this dearth of aspiration Professor Mick Waters, a former Director of Curriculum at the

---

[7] Gilby et al *National Survey of parents and Children: family Life, Aspirations and Engagement with learning* (2008) Dept. for Education,

[8] Ross, A. *Disengagement from Education among 14-16 year olds* (2009)

[9] Wills et al *What Did You Do in School Today?* (2009) Canadian Educational Association

[10] Student surveys cited on www.thefuturesproject.org

UK government's Qualifications and Curriculum Authority once said to me, 'Too many of us expect learning to be like a cold shower – if it isn't hurting, it isn't doing you any good'.

The real problem with student engagement on a social level is that the numbers of visibly disengaged represent just the tip of the iceberg. Many students fall into a category, described to me by one UK teacher, as 'radiator kids' (not doing much except keeping the room warm); still others are classified as 'disengaged achievers,' gaining good grades, but emotionally disinvested in their learning.

Internationally, student engagement is unevenly distributed. Engagement has dramatically fallen in countries, like England and the United States, where anxiety over 'international competitiveness' has led to a deadening emphasis upon high-stakes national standardised testing. In these countries, many kids view schools, not as places of exploration, but as exam factories.

The irony is that student outcomes improve in those countries where a greater emphasis upon engagement goes alongside a lessening of importance on high-stakes testing. As writer Alfie Kohn has noted, 'when interest appears, achievement usually follows'.[11]

The Best Days Of Your Life?
Should we be concerned about students becoming increasingly disengaged, especially if they're gaining the qualifications needed to find a job? Well, even if you accept that passing school exams and getting a degree will enable them to get good jobs – which as we've seen must now be in some doubt – the unintended 'side effect' of this processing of students to become

11 Kohn, A. *The Schools Our Children Deserve* (1999) Houghton Mifflin

achieving, not engaged, learners, is to kill off a love of learning. American educators label this 'drilling and killing'.

Disengaged students become disengaged employees – or non-employed. In 2011, the UK figure for people aged 16-24 not in employment, education or training (NEETS) was over one million – the highest since records were kept.[12] This represents one in five young people, and includes 10 percent (and steadily rising) that possess the qualifications needed to go to university, but have chosen not to apply.

Conversely, a recent longitudinal Australian study – one of the few to focus upon engagement in school – found that engagement was a key determinant of student success 20 years later: 'The more children felt connected to their school community and felt engaged, rather than bored, the greater their likelihood of achieving a higher educational qualification and going on to a professional or managerial career.'[13]

Instead of regarding disengagement in school as an inevitable feature of adolescent angst, we should see it for what it really is: a shocking waste of young potential which has lifelong consequences. Sadly, rather than becoming intentional about engagement, too many education leaders waste time working out which lever to pull to force teachers and students to do more, work harder, while teachers waste time coming up with ways to deflect blame. And, at the end of the line, those to whom learning is done waste time pretending to be interested. A visionary principal at an outstanding Australian primary school once shared a comment from one of her brighter students. When he was asked what school had taught him, he replied that the most important thing he'd learned was 'how to fall asleep with my eyes open'.

---

12 *NEET Statistics* (2011) UK Dept. for Education
13 *'School engagement predicts success later in life'* TheConversation.com

And yet, if we could prioritise engagement in school we might finally address one of the most intractable of social problems: the so-called 'achievement gap'. Repeated surveys have suggested that a child's life chances are predominantly shaped, not by their education, but by their postcode location. The Australian study quoted earlier, however, found that, 'children's interest and engagement in school influences their prospects of educational and occupational success 20 years later, over and above their academic attainment and socio-economic background'.

In other words, an engaged student, from a disadvantaged background, is likely to have better life chances than a disengaged child from a better-off background. It's hard to understand, in the light of this kind of evidence, why policy makers aren't more interested in engagement in school.

The social and economic costs of student and employee disengagement should have us all worried. The linkage between employee engagement and company performance is irrefutable. But students who are disengaged from school are likely not simply to be disengaged from work, but from civic society too.

It's not just quarterly sales figures that are affected by falling levels of engagement. The glue that holds our societies together is dependent upon our finding ways to re-engage our students, our employees and our citizens.

Why Engaging Learning Environments Matter

So far we've seen that the combined forces of disintermediation, globalisation, long-term recovery from the global financial crisis and the transfer of economic power from west to east, have profound consequences for us all. Previous certainties have become dangerously unstable. We are simultaneously fearful, disengaged and nervous about the future.

We need hardly make matters worse, by driving the enjoyment out of earning a living or going to school. And yet that is precisely what we're doing, by trusting employees and students less, by eroding their scope for independent thought and actions, and by not attaching sufficient importance to engagement, and learning.

The places where formal learning and training takes place need to adopt open principles and recognise the critical importance of engagement in, *and through*, learning. The overwhelming majority of our businesses still see learning as something delivered by qualified 'trainers' in places that still look like classrooms. Meanwhile, our truly innovative companies have long understood that, as Harold Jarche observed, 'Work is Learning and Learning is the Work', and are reaping the rewards as a result.

Political and social upheaval, of the kind we are living through, often creates the breeding grounds for a new generation of visionaries. The counter-culture of the 1960s and 1970s produced the likes of Steve Jobs, Bill Gates and Tim Berners-Lee who irrevocably changed the way we work, play and communicate. I believe the visionaries of the future are likely to emerge from the kind of environments where learning is collaborative, social, passion-led and values-driven, networked, horizontal, democratic and creative.

We have to abandon the antiquated, enclosed learning systems upon which we currently rely and seek to engage the young social activists, entrepreneurs and technologists of today in re-imagining the open systems of tomorrow. And fast.

Chapter Six

Open Learning in Society

The central argument informing this book is that if we are to make business and education more innovative, more effective, we need to learn from the values and actions present when groups are doing things for themselves. The enthusiasm and ability of small groups of self-organising citizens to respond to challenges makes bigger, better funded, organisations look slow and cumbersome in comparison.

They're more open, lighter on their feet, and they learn fast. They bring the participation, purpose and passion outlined in Chapter Four to complex problems. Critically, they don't separate learning from doing. They gain knowledge *through* collaborative action, and the results of their actions determine what they need to know next.

Most of us experienced formal learning like this: you were required to be seated, while someone told you things, without the value of context or purpose. You were assessed on your understanding of that knowledge not through demonstrating a skill or putting that knowledge to use, but purely through recall or reasoning.

The illustrations I'm about to share are polar opposites of that experience. They suggest that it's in the application of knowledge that the learning power resides. We learn best when we build things, fix things or provide a service to others.

Collectively solving problems provides not only the motivation to learn, but also the springboard to further learning.

Surviving Sandy

When Hurricane Sandy hit the north-east coastline of America, in October 2012, a nation held its breath and waited for the government response. President Barack Obama and New York City Mayor Michael Bloomberg were acutely aware of the failure, seven years earlier, to respond adequately to Hurricane Katrina. This time, the media reports were more favourable. President Obama was considered to have handled the response of the Federal Emergency Management Agency (FEMA) far better than George W. Bush had done in 2005.

On the ground, however, reports were less congratulatory. People complained of supply chain problems: food, water and clothing filled warehouses but were not being distributed quickly or evenly. Worse, in the months following the storm, FEMA was accused of overcomplicating the aid application process, and unfairly rejecting 'untold' numbers of applications.

Because of its proximity to the 2012 Presidential Election, the scale of the devastation caused by Sandy was under-reported compared with that of Katrina. The numbers were dramatic: 72 deaths; over 7 million people left without power; 346,000 homes damaged or destroyed; 100,000 jobs lost and an estimated damage bill of $71bn.

Although federal disaster relief was lacking, Hurricane Sandy provoked a self-organised response from tens of thousands of ordinary people, marshalled by voluntary groups like Recovers.org. First established in 2011, by Caitria and Morgan O'Neill after a freak tornado hit their hometown in Massachusetts, Recovers manages volunteers, tracks donations and serves as an information hub. In the seven days after

Hurricane Sandy made landfall, over 23,000 volunteers signed up to Recovers.org.

But this was just one self-organised response. Almost overnight, a slew of groups appeared: 'New York Communities for Change', 'Rebuild Staten Island Foundation' (which helped repair over 1,000 uninsured homes), 'Rockaway Help', and many others all took to Facebook to provide volunteers to help clean up the mess.

Perhaps the most effective action group, however, was 'Occupy Sandy Recovery'. Staffed by many of the same people who had taken part in the Occupy Wall Street protests, it was no surprise that Occupy volunteers were the first to set up food stations and distribution centres. They'd had lots of practise looking after people in the Zuccotti Park encampment in 2011, though admittedly not on the scale that Sandy presented.

Coordinating the distribution of food, clothing and donations was only part of the 'mutual aid network' that Occupy established. They mobilised over 50,000 volunteers – more than the military presence in the immediate aftermath of the hurricane – to pump water, remove mould, shift debris and rebuild homes. Almost exactly a year after being forcibly evicted from a New York park, Occupy volunteers were back on the streets. And they stuck around long after the initial emergency to help restore life to large areas of the city.

But it wasn't just the inside of people's homes that they were restoring. Sandy Recovery restored the reputation of the Occupy movement in the eyes of New Yorkers. As Roz Mays, a fitness instructor who volunteered to work at one of their five New York centres, confessed:

"To be quite honest I thought the Occupy Wall Street movement were crazy hippies. Turns out they are phenomenal in transforming communities. This is a home-grown community based organisation of people who just want to help".

Tellingly, the Occupy Sandy website carried more than details of how to 'respond and rebuild'. Its library section encouraged people to share their views on climate change and disaster capitalism, and their Storyline project allowed people to express traumatised feelings in the wake of the disaster, through personal testimonies. People who came out of apartments to direct traffic when the traffic lights went down; musicians who ran workshops in emergency shelters; women who cycled energy bikes, so that mobile phones could be recharged after power blackouts.

Though learning was less of a priority than helping others, those engaged in Occupy Sandy and Storyline, embarked upon a steep learning curve. They learned about climate change; emergency sanitation; community cohesion; post-trauma stress; alternative power sources; disaster management – the list is extensive. They learned how to put together powerful oral histories, and how to present the Occupy movement as a grass-roots self-help community in ways that weren't in evidence in 2011. This was learning through doing writ large.

The personal stories of the Sandy Recovery paints a moving picture of what people can do to help themselves when public support services cannot cope. They also rekindle a lost sense of community. Some of the storytellers remarked on how they felt 'kind of sad when it was all over, and we went back into our homes'. The Global Learning Commons is at its best when confronted with an emergency.

Just Do It

If the English Riots of 2011 were part of the wake-up call to make civic participation a higher priority, then a less-publicised

105

aspect of the riots helped show how that aspiration could be realised. After seeing TV pictures of a furniture store ablaze in Croydon on 8th August 2011, artist and writer, Dan Thompson, urged people to volunteer to help clean up the damage done. I was working at my laptop the following morning, and in the midst of a national mood of gloom and foreboding, something truly remarkable happened.

By mid-morning tweets with the hashtag '#riotcleanup' were coming in thick and fast, with people volunteering in their tens of thousands. The hashtag became the second most active worldwide. One image in particular – a shot of hundreds of brooms being held aloft in a London street – was re-tweeted globally, and the 'Broom Army' achieved iconic status within an hour.

Politicians were quick to seize on the opportunity. Boris Johnson, Mayor of London, was photographed pushing a broom, and Prime Minister David Cameron later referred to the campaign in his speech to the Conservative Party Conference:

"Dan Thompson watched the riots unfold on television. But he didn't sit there and say 'the council will clean it up'. He got on the internet. He sent out a call. And with others, he started a social movement. People picked up their brooms and reclaimed their streets."

Despite these fairly crude attempts to gain some reflected political glory from Dan's idea, Cameron was right to describe what happened as a 'social movement'. Without requiring permission from anyone, over 100,000 showed their immediate support for the clean-up via Twitter, and thousands of people turned out to clean up the mess that the rioters had caused.

Furthermore, #riotcleanup acted as a catalyst for a range of similar campaigns: #reverseriots, #riotrebuild and

#peckhampeacewall were some examples of ordinary people contributing time and support to help restore the fractured sense of community. The government response was to hastily pass the Riot Damages Act, which sought to compensate victims of the riots. When it failed to get compensation for those who needed it most, however, these social movements stepped in to raise money to get shops and businesses open again.

I was curious to discover Dan Thompson's expectations for the clean-up campaign, and what people had learned from becoming involved:

"I aimed for 50 (out of around 4,000) of my followers to respond. I knew they were interested in local shops and independent traders and used language that would engage that audience. I think people learned that you can do small things and make a big impact; that you can take action in your local community and that tools like Twitter are useful for organising. They learned that actions don't have to have a big investment in either planning or resources to have an impact."

Dan's campaign reached many times more than the 50 volunteers he hoped for, and is a striking example of what I call the six imperatives powering the Global Learning Commons. So far, we've looked at characteristics and principles that shape the Global Learning Commons (participation, passion and purpose) and the values and actions that determine the learning (share, open, free, trust).

But principles and values aren't enough to become 'open' – you need to have motivation for deep and powerful learning to happen. The following are the motivational drivers behind the phenomenal innovation seen in social learning, and help explain why such innovation is largely lacking in schools, colleges and the workplace. These imperatives don't rely on external incentives (financial reward or career promotion) but are instead exclusively intrinsic in how they fire us up:

- Do it yourself
- Do it now
- Do it with friends
- Do unto others
- Do it for fun
- Do it for the world to see

Although I've assigned some examples of innovative learning to specific 'Do-its', it's worth pointing out that most of the examples which follow combine more than one imperative. Indeed many, like Dan's #riotcleanup, combine all six.

Do It Yourself (Autonomy)

The desire to take initiative and responsibility in the social space is key to understanding what has made social learning so compelling. We are beginning to realise that we don't have to wait for those who govern locally or nationally to act on our behalf. We now have the means to act autonomously, in many areas of our social lives and it makes us feel better about ourselves, and others, when we do. It's where self-determinism meets collaboration, accelerated by social networking tools.

The headline-grabbers are well known. Social movements like Amnesty International, Greenpeace and Avaaz have millions of supporters who may be asked to take actions ranging from signing an online petition to forming life-risking human barricades. Their independence comes largely through steering clear of complex political affiliations, opting instead for single-issue, single-objective protests.

Avaaz has over 25 million members, in almost every country on the planet. Its membership has risen eight-fold in just five years. Every day or so, I receive an email that informs me of some aspect of geo-politics: everything from human rights to environmental disasters. I am often asked to sign a global petition, seeking action from governments around the world. Like most members, I make it my business to understand the cause I am putting my name to. My learning derives from wanting to be a responsible citizen. Although it appeals directly to the individual, Avaaz encapsulates what it calls 'the rising ethic of global interdependence'. So, when, in October 2011, a highly contentious bill giving the US government the right to effectively censor the internet was introduced to the House of Representatives, Avaaz mobilised 3 million signatures from around the world, which led to a meeting at the White House. The bill, by now widely discredited, was quietly shelved in January 2012.

Perhaps the two most widely-cited examples of DIY are the creation of the open source software operating system, Linux, and the online encyclopedia, Wikipedia. In both instances there was, and continues to be, a desire to contribute knowledge, irrespective of rank or status, which is then built-upon, critiqued, or corrected by others. Both produced outstanding products, which the world has gratefully used at no cost.

More recently, DIY is attempting to get us to think and act differently in our everyday lives. 'We Are What We Do' is a good example. It began as a Christmas book placed at the checkout in Sainsbury supermarkets. 'Change the World for a Fiver' featured a collection of simple actions, which can have social or environmental impact. 'We Are What We Do' became an online hub, where individuals could post ideas for others to act upon. 'Start a car pool', 'learn more, do more', may not be as dramatic as protesting in Tahrir Square, but such actions have, at the time of writing, led to over five million 'actions'. *'We Are What We Do'* is now a not-for-profit 'behaviour change' company that creates ways for millions of people to do more, small, good things.

Do It Now (Immediacy)

I've noted, earlier, the emerging force of 'Just-In-Time' learning. Lilian Katz, a distinguished early childhood educator, highlights the link between immediacy and one of the most contentious labels in formal education: 'relevance'. Katz coined the term 'horizontal relevance', to suggest that learning is most powerful when the learner acquires a piece of information to solve an immediate problem.

Its opposite, according to Katz, is 'vertical relevance', when the information might be needed at some unspecified point in the future. This form of learning is 'Just-In-Case' (it comes up on the test paper). Vertical relevance still determines most teaching, or work-placed training. Bored learners would sooner call it vertically irrelevant, since they often fail to see the point of what's being taught.

There's nothing more guaranteed to raise the hackles of a traditionalist than the R-word. They equate a responsibility for making learning relevant with 'pandering' to students. They also argue that we can't always predict what we'll need to know, so the relevance question is, well, irrelevant. It's true that some learning – the dreaded health and safety training for instance – is best done in advance, and not while the fire is raging. But there's a reason why you get the airline safety briefing when the engines are running, and you're buckled-up, and not when you're booking your ticket.

I could, and frequently do, argue all day with traditionalists about immediacy and relevance, but that's not the point. Because what's happening when people learn informally is that everything they seek out is horizontally relevant, whether it's the guitar chord you want your elder brother to show you, so you can play your favourite song, or the video of how to cook chicken chasseur for tonight's dinner. So, whatever we think doesn't really matter, I'm afraid. They're bound to want formal learning to be more like that. It's just the way the world is.

There's another reason why immediacy matters. Research in neuroscience suggests that every time you post a request on Twitter for a particular reference, or news report you missed, and you get an immediate response, you get a little dopamine hit.[1] It turns out that finding information that provides a quick solution to a problem helps 'stamp' the memory in our brain and 'attaches motivational importance to otherwise neutral environmental stimuli'. In other words, Just-In-Time learning is more likely to stick, while Just-In-Case learning is Teflon-coated.

For those who've always delivered learning in orderly, sequential blocks, and who yearn for acquiring knowledge for its own sake, the random ad-hocery of the Do It Now imperative is a pretty tough pill to swallow. Swallow it they must, however, because, out there in society's Global Learning Commons, learners are frolicking around, being delighted by the learning power of now. And they are increasingly expecting those dopamine hits in the classroom, or training room, too.

Do It With Friends (Collegiality)

Formal education and training likes to frame learning as an individual pursuit. This is sometimes because it's easier to measure it that way, and we only value what we can measure. It's also the case that the historically preferred method of transferring knowledge, from the expert to the learner, has always been one-to-one, individual tuition.

---

[1] Wise, R. *Dopamine, Learning and Motivation*, Nature Reviews Neuroscience 5, June 2004

In the Global Learning Commons, it's a very different picture. We have followers, friends and personal learning networks. We read daily online newspapers, automatically aggregated to include people whose knowledge we admire. Learning here is networked, linked-in and highly social.

While we may never meet the people we now learn from, it's wrong to dismiss these relationships as imaginary. Communications may be geographically stretched, but they're far from distant. It's appropriately called a social network. My initial perception of Twitter was that it was little more than electronic attention-seeking. If one were simply to judge it by newspaper regurgitation of celebrity tweets, such prejudices would be confirmed. My fairly limited personal learning network was transformed, however, once I started using it. And I'm not alone.

Millions of workers now consider Twitter an indispensable, if not primary, source of professional development. Fluid learning communities regularly come together for 'hashtag meet-ups', where issues are debated with no one person able to hog the conversation, due to the 140-character limit. People learn stuff, but they also share the small talk of friends.

John Seeley Brown has written about the learning patterns of a group of extreme aerial surfers living near his house in Maui, Hawaii. These five friends have, remarkably, all become world champion surfers, on an island that hitherto had failed to produce any. Seeley Brown observed how they formed an intense community of practice, built around their respect and affection for each other.

Training sessions were recorded on video, and then critiqued. Adjacent disciplines like skateboarding and motocross were mined for new moves, classic competitions analysed. As a study group, it was about as good as it gets. Indeed, the global surfing community benefits from a highly-effective learning commons that has formed around a mix of attitudes, behaviours, values and practices. It has done this in sharp contrast, and perhaps in response to, the commercial exploitation of surf culture.

Seeley Brown highlights the 'tinkering' at the heart of surfing. Experimentation, risk-taking, innovation (and building upon previous innovations) lie at the heart of tinkering. There are similarities here with the notion of 'hacking' – in the benign sense. The hacker community identifies five core beliefs: sharing, openness, decentralisation, free access to computers and world improvement.[2]

If one substitutes 'the ocean' for 'computers', then it's likely most surfers would subscribe to these principles. The two communities also share a common desire to offer an alternative way of living, being comfortable with the mantle of 'outsiders'. It seems that this combination of resistance and purpose has contributed to their effectiveness as learners.

In researching this book, I became fascinated by surfers as a learning community. I travelled to one of the most beautiful places on earth, Byron Bay, in Northern New South Wales in Australia, to interview Rusty Miller. Here's a man who can justifiably be called a surfing legend. Born in Southern California, Rusty became USA surfing champion in 1965.

Since then he travelled the world in search of surfing challenges, but became disenchanted with the industry that grew up around the sport. In the 1970s he discovered Byron Bay and decided to set up one of the world's first surf schools there. Now in his late 60s (but with the body of a 30-year-old) Rusty teaches beginner surfers every day. He is not just a great coach, he's a great educator. He acknowledges the importance of mentoring, in his case gained by hanging out with lifeguards:

---

[2] Levy, S. *Hackers: Heroes of the Computer Revolution*, (1984) Anchor Press

"I can't remember them saying 'do this' or 'do that', but they'd look out for me. I just went out with them. If it was too big, they'd say 'oh, you can't go out'."

He also recognises the importance of personalisation in learning, and the need for learning to be understood in context:

"I'm getting really good at assessing where people are at. People learn differently. There's a mental attitude about learning that you can assess, by talking to them, it could be something simple like "This guy doesn't feel good about himself." So there's a relationship between their attitude and what I see them physically doing."

Crucially, Rusty shares the same approaches as Maui's champion surfers, in learning from 'adjacencies' – in Rusty's case, philosophy and the ecology of the ocean – and through an appreciation that the best teachers are the best learners:

"I'm still excited about it, because I'm learning so much. It's like the clerk in Canterbury Tales...'and gladly will he learn, and gladly teach'. That's why I'm so stoked."

I'm convinced that Chaucer himself would be stoked to be quoted by a surfing legend, and that there's much to be learned about innovation and learning itself from analysing surfers as a community of practice. There must be a research grant in there somewhere.

Do Unto Others (Generosity)

When one looks at the explosion of groups now forming to help others in recent times, it sometimes feels like we were sedated into believing we were bad people, and that an awakening is starting to take place.

I know that last sentence sounds like it came from the musical 'Hair', but consider this: if, in a pre-internet age, someone proposed that we should open our houses up to complete strangers and that these visitors would expect us, not simply to feed them, but to escort them around our cities, they would have been given pretty short shrift.

I've already highlighted the success of Couchsurfing.com – but there are others: Hospitality Club, GlobalFreeloaders, BeWelcome. And then there are the plethora of fundraising and donation sites, like Kickstarter and JustGiving.com. It turns out we're not so bad, after all. Who knew?

After the success of #riotcleanup, Dan Thompson launched 'We Will Gather' in 2012. It's a way of connecting people with free time and a desire to volunteer with actions in their area. All that is needed, according to the website, is 'a good thing that needs to be done, a place for people to meet up, and a date and time'. Although many of the actions are small – cleaning civic spaces, or fixing up gardens – the intentions behind them are profound. We were supposed to be driven by self-interest, encapsulated in Margaret Thatcher's famous quote, 'There is no such thing as society, only individual men and women'. Quite clearly, she got that wrong.

Marcia Conner, co-author of 'The New Social Learning', highlights the impact that social media has upon the spirit, and acts, of volunteering:

"Social learning thrives in a culture of service and wonder...accelerated when we give our attention to individuals, groups and projects that interest and energize us. We self-select the themes we want to follow and filter out those that feel burdensome, all with impunity."

In other words, we're no longer likely to face a knock on the door, asking for help from church or community, to carry out actions that fail to inspire us. There are now so many projects and causes looking for help that we can surely find ones that we can identify with and commit to with enthusiasm, rather than through a sense of duty.

There has been a long tradition of 'service learning' in North American schools and it usually makes for memorable learning and motivated learners. As schools have become more like enclosures, however, the opportunities to connect with local neighbourhoods have shrunk at precisely the same time as such opportunities are exponentially growing in our social spaces. We learn best when we do it with passion and purpose. Doing unto others as we'd have them do to ourselves provides a powerful motivation to learn.

Do It For Fun (Playfulness)

Conditioned by years of dreary copying from the blackboard, most of us developed low expectations of the pleasure to be found in learning. Yet, this was only ever true for formal education. When we're with friends or family, there's simply no point to learning if we don't enjoy it. Having fun is the primary driver.

Does that mean that the learning that is taking place is somehow inferior? I don't think so. Some of the most important life skills we master are achieved only because of the pleasure derived along the way. Learning to swim, or to ride a bicycle, are good examples.

Fun without challenge, however, is usually an unsatisfying experience. I've played golf most of my adult life. I enjoy playing, but I probably enjoy practising even more. Why? Because no one ever masters the ability to hit a golf ball consistently well, not even the best pros. Understanding the physics, and biomechanics, involved in bringing a club head to hit a golf ball perfectly square to the target line at just the right angle of elevation and at the optimum point of acceleration... well, it's a lifelong challenge. But the feeling of hitting just one pure shot, that seems to fly effortlessly off the clubface, out of maybe 20 scrappy ones, is enough to keep me working at it.

It's what the MIT professor, Seymour Papert, calls 'hard fun': the potent mix of challenge and enjoyment. Writing in an article in 2002, Papert acknowledged the difficulty in finding the space between criticising traditional schooling's coercive approach to learning, and joining the 'touchy feely, let's make it fun, let's make it easy' school of engagement. Papert's concept of hard fun arose from the words of an 8th-grader:

> "A teacher heard one child using these words to describe the computer work: 'It's fun. It's hard. It's Logo (the programming language being learned).' I have no doubt that this kid called the work fun because it was hard rather than in spite of being hard."[3]

For some reason, learning and fun have become incompatible. Students aren't there to have fun. If they were, school wouldn't need to be compulsory. Having fun at school means students aren't being stretched, doesn't it? But Papert's fun comes directly through being challenged, having previous beliefs contradicted, tackling difficult problems. Hard fun is something that all learning professionals should strive to create.

Society has an often-contradictory relationship with the enjoyment derived from computers. On the one hand, we (the concerned parents) understand the importance of computer

---

[3] Papert, S. *Hard Fun* (2002) Bangor Daily News

competence in our children. But we also exhibit a kind of protestant prurience when we think our children may be spending too much time having fun playing video games. In 1981, British Labour MP, George Foulkes drafted a bill, 'Control of Space Invaders (and other Electronic Games) Bill' out of concern for Space Invaders' addictiveness and potential for causing 'deviancy'. The bill was defeated by only 20 votes. Seriously, we almost banned Space Invaders.

To be fair, there have been deaths caused by exhaustion, or cardiac arrest, due to video gamers in China and South Korea playing video games for 50-hour stretches. These, however, are isolated cases, and the challenge for learning professionals is to harness the engagement, self-discipline and resilience shown in a gamer striving to complete a level, to more conventional learning situations. Enter 'serious gaming'.

Serious gaming is a generic term for video gaming with a more overt educational purpose. After initially struggling for credibility – the term was at first seen as oxymoronic – recent studies have provided convincing evidence of the cognitive impact of serious gaming.

The most striking example of serious gaming is FoldIt.[4] Devised by the University of Washington, FoldIt enables thousands of gamers to solve science problems specifically relating to 'protein folding', predicting the shapes which amino acids will form in HIV, Aids, Cancer and Alzheimer's.

Zoran Popovich, one of FoldIt's creators says that the game has shown 'that it is possible to create experts in a particular domain purely through game play'. One of its leading players is Scott Zaccanelli, a massage therapist from Dallas, Texas. Players are ranked according to their ability to figure out problems.

---

[4] www.fold.it/portal

Zaccanelli himself plays for a couple of hours every evening and, at the time of writing, is ranked 12th in the world:

> "Everybody's got their motivations for it. Some do it for the camaraderie, others for the competition. (I'm just) happy that science is being done."

If you're new to video gaming, this might all seem a bit nerdy. Maybe, but you should know that one of FoldIt's 2012's puzzles was to identify a folded-protein structure, made by HIV monkeys, which had eluded scientists for 15 years. Scott's team was able to work it out in 10 days. Does that sound like fun?

Do It For The World To See (High visibility)

The Global Learning Commons allows one insight to be shared among millions. In April 2012, Martha Payne, a nine-year-old student from Lochgilphead, Scotland, began blogging about her school dinners, posting a daily photograph of her lunch. Martha intends to be a journalist, so was encouraged by her father to write about her food. Because some of the portion sizes were shockingly small, word of Martha's blog, 'NeverSeconds', soon spread.

The local authority instructed Martha to stop blogging. One might have thought that a better response would have been to ask why kids were going hungry at school. Celebrity chef and food campaigner Jamie Oliver tweeted Martha's blog and virality ensued. Suitably chastened, the local authority dropped its ban and did something about their school dinners. Six months later, NeverSeconds had reached almost nine million page views and Martha's first book had been published, with the proceeds from each book now providing a daily meal for 25 children in Malawi.

It's an extraordinary story, but one which has become rather more commonplace, due to the irrepressible rise of citizen journalism. Podcasting, blogging, tweeting – we are all journalists now. And it can be captivating – if you tweet it, they will come. User-generated content is transforming not just how we watch television – YouTube has forced all major TV broadcasters to offer viewing-on-demand – but also what we watch. Although we now take it for granted, pretty much every news broadcast, on every station, in every country around the world now routinely incorporates footage from citizen journalists. Our knowledge of what is happening around the world would be infinitely poorer without it.

Campaign groups have been quick to exploit the power of social media, none more so than the Invisible Children group who, on 5th March 2012, released 'KONY 2012', a powerfully emotive video (though flawed in its accuracy), detailing the atrocities carried out by Joseph Kony on young children in Uganda and the Democratic Republic of Congo. The video had over 100 million views in its first week, making it the biggest viral video in the history of the internet.

Whatever one's views of the campaign – to have global leaders significantly ramp up their efforts to capture the Lord's Resistance Army leader before the end of 2012 – there was no disputing the impact of the video in the Global Learning Commons. It may have ultimately failed in its primary ambition to capture Kony in 2012, but it raised awareness of the issue, and animated young people around the globe.

Here's just one example, of which there must have been thousands: I watched the video in Australia on the day of its release, and was sufficiently moved by it to write a blog post. A history teacher, Neal Watkin, at Coplestone High School, Suffolk, read the post and shared the video with his students. Within hours I'd received an email from Neal telling me that students had formed an 'action committee' to see how they could help the campaign. Others, sceptical of some of the claims made in the video, conducted their own research. A week later I received a message from Neal:

"The action committee met and started to plan some action. One big idea was to reproduce the Kony video, but using our own students. It has turned into a great teaching point as we have been able to explore the issues of Uganda in the classroom and through impromptu sessions in the corridor. Tomorrow we will set up an online space to collect ideas and actions. Not sure yet whether we will follow Kony 2012 campaign or do something else to support Ugandan child soldiers. However, the campaign has helped raise awareness."

Critics of KONY 2012 have argued that impressionable young people would have been falsely informed by the video's naivety. This typically underestimates young people's ability to make up their own minds. A fierce debate raged on YouTube, presenting all sides of the story. I believe most kids would have responded in the same way as the Coplestone students, and sought more information. My point here is that the phenomenal rise in the production, not simply consumption, of media whether video, blogging or tweeting may sometimes seem like the self-aggrandisement of the self-opinionated. But the potential of an unlimited audience for young students' work can also transform our motivation to learn. Vimeo, YouTube and Twitter are filled with examples of extraordinary student work, where the public assessment means far more to these young people than whether they got a B+ from their teacher.

*****

So, these are the six imperatives that propel motivation in the Global Learning Commons. I should stress that these 'Do-its' are morally neutral. It's possible to see the activities of 'hacktivist' organisations like Anonymous or LulzSec as either fighting for all our freedoms of information, or irresponsibly putting internal securities at risk. But, whatever one thinks of their ethics, there is no denying their ability to learn, innovate, and collaborate. Their capacity to temporarily bring major corporations to the point of collapse, as they did following Sony's support for the Stop Online Piracy Act, is disproportionate to their size of membership.

That they have largely evaded the clutches of a phalanx of internal security forces around the world, speaks volumes about the innovative learning environment they have created. It seems to me that there have to be powerful imperatives underlying their activities, at least some of which I've identified here.

While these motivations can be used for harm as well as good, it should be apparent that, overwhelmingly, people who are learning socially outside the workplace and formal education do so out of a sense of altruism. The technology provides the tools, but it's the power of personal connections, informal learning and displaying generosity to one another, which creates the imperative to learn, and act, collaboratively.

The Global Learning Commons is at its most powerful in the social space, and the illustrations I've chosen – community activism, play-based learning, online collaboration, serious gaming, tacit and informal learning, and self-publishing – do not even begin to represent the ingenuity, innovation and optimism out there. The question that underpins this book is whether the richness and vibrancy of learning approaches, which we see socially, can be brought into more formal arenas. And if so, what are the environments we need to create, and the values and actions we need to foster?

Chapter Seven

Open Learning at Work

Part One: Learning-Powered Innovation

On the evening of 1st February 1880, Charles Clarke, a young civil engineering graduate, began his first day's work at a factory complex in rural New Jersey. To start a new job on a Sunday evening was somewhat unusual, but Clarke was willing to do just about anything to earn a living. The United States was only just seeing the end of the 'long depression', triggered by the financial crisis known as the 'Panic of 1873'. Since the depression brought the expansion of the railroads to an abrupt stop, Clarke had done a succession of unfulfilling jobs.

Whatever hopes he may have had about his new job, he must have been disappointed with the starting salary: $12 a week, and significantly less than the $20 a week he'd received in his last job, teaching at a school in Philadelphia. He must have also been quite taken aback by the working practices, which must have seemed anarchic. America's manufacturing industry was in the grip of the 'scientific management' methods of Frederick Winslow Taylor. Efficiency, standardisation, elimination of waste, were key drivers in the shift from craft production to mass production.

Clarke's boss, a scruffily-dressed and dynamic man in his early thirties, had other ideas. Charles' arrival coincided with a midnight feast, with hampers laid around the pipe organ the owner had installed to encourage regular sing-songs. In the initial few weeks of his employment, he would be asked to support a wide variety of tasks: one minute his hands were drafting designs, the next, thick with grease, fixing machines.

Job descriptions were non-existent – most of the young men who had recently joined the company were labelled 'muckers' (an English slang term), available to do whatever the boss ordered, and were frequently found to be 'mucking about', verbally abusing each other, indulging in practical jokes, occasionally giving each other electric shocks.

The boss, who despite his age was known affectionately as 'the old man', expected a minimum of 60 hours per week, from the muckers, though 80-hour weeks were not uncommon. Recognising the pressure of such arduous work, he regularly organised impromptu fishing trips and drinking sessions for his 20 or so employees, and was the first to roll up his sleeves when experiments went on all-night.

Unsurprisingly, the long hours and constantly changing roles took its toll, and staff turnover, in 1880, was 50 percent. But Charles Clarke was never happier. Writing about the 'little community of kindred spirits' he remarked, 'I was constantly observant of all that was going on about me working and studying overtime, as the ambitious young should ever do if they expect to move onward and upward.'[1]

Francis Upton, Clarke's old college pal, was responsible for getting Clarke his job. He clearly felt he was back at college too, writing to his father, 'I find my work very pleasant here and not much different from the time when I was a student. The strangest

---

[1] B.S. Finn, *Working at Menlo Park*, in *Working at Inventing* ed W. S. Pretzer (1989) John Hopkins University Press; *Charles L. Clarke at Menlo Park in 1880* in *Menlo Park Reminiscences Part 2* (2002) Kessinger Publ.

thing to me is that the $12 I get each Saturday for my labor does not seem like work, but like study and I enjoy it'.

As you may have guessed halfway through that description (where else were workers giving each other electric shocks in 1880?) the 'old man' was Thomas Edison, and the factory was Edison's Menlo Park hamlet in New Jersey. I've begun this section on how the Global Learning Commons can host the dynamic workplace to remind us that innovative learning environments didn't just appear overnight in Silicon Valley start-ups. Indeed, I can think of no better setting for the values, actions and motivations behind 'open' than those found in Menlo Park during the six years that Edison set up his 'inventions factory' there, from 1876 to 1882.

It's worth reminding ourselves of the prodigious innovation and productivity of that small group of men. In those six years over 400 patents were filed, creating products which shaped the 20th century: the invention of the phonograph, the carbon telephone transmitter, stations which could generate and transmit electricity, and the incandescent light bulb. It's hard to imagine how the past century would have been without the entrepreneurship and innovation of a man who has, with some justification, been labelled 'the father of inventions'.

What the Inventions Factory Tells Us Today

It's a testimony to Thomas Edison's vision and imagination that we still look to his life and work for inspiration. And many of the leading creative workplaces of the past 50 years, including Google, Facebook, 3M, have sought to emulate the innovative culture of Edison Labs.

Edison's success was built on the realisation that innovation could only flourish in a learning environment shaped by collaboration and curiosity. Despite the phenomenal number of patents filed, Edison asked to be judged, not on his successes, but by the number of experiments carried out each day. In contrast to many present-day organisations, innovation at Menlo Park was powered by learning, not a need to find more customers, or to create a return on investment.

This was no solitary wizard – his ability to find and attract talent, and his skill in creating a dynamic learning environment was Edison's real genius.   What can we learn from the culture and structure of Menlo Park? I believe there are five key ingredients, listed below, together with some contemporary manifestations:

1. Create A Machine-Shop Culture

Menlo Park was known as the 'inventions factory'. Its naming was intentional, bringing together the head (having the idea) and the hands (making it work) – creativity and craftsmanship. Most companies do one well, but rarely both. Edison fashioned a learning culture where head and hands were equals. In doing so, he imported the practices he'd seen in the machine shops in Newark, New Jersey.

A machine-shop culture is built around the concept that the craft and skill of the artisan needs to be nurtured and supported. The work was organised, monitored and managed to give dignity, value and independence to the work of the 'muckers', and everyone was expected to 'muck in' and get their hands dirty.

However, in addition to affording equal respect to intellectual and practical pursuits, there are values you'd want to have in place, if you want to build a machine-shop culture:

a) Flatten Structures – Looking at photographs taken inside the machine shop at Menlo Park, it's virtually impossible to tell which one is Edison. 'Lead experimenters' held no particular authority over 'muckers'. Edison knew that good ideas could come from anywhere, and that creativity hates hierarchy.

b) Encourage unorthodoxy – The rigid working practices emerging through the industrial age, held no attraction to Edison or his workers. 'Nine-to-five' frequently meant working through the night and sleeping the following day. Acutely aware that they were making history, the culture had to foster counter-intuition. Menlo Park's modern-day equivalent is probably MIT's Media Lab, where inventions include E ink (which made digital book readers possible) the $100 laptop used in the 'One Laptop Per Child' programme, and the hologram used in your credit card. They have a long tradition of encouraging unorthodoxy. Writing about its formation in 1979, Media Lab's Chair, Nicholas Negroponte, notes: 'New ideas would emerge from a heterogeneous collection of edgy, unorthodox people...those people came from various parts of MIT, from architecture to physics, from music to maths. In some cases those faculties were no longer welcome in their home departments. In that sense, the founding faculty was a veritable Salon des Refusés. Misfits'.[2]

c) Welcome diversity – Negroponte suggests that the Media Lab is 'anti-disciplinary', that even the notion of a 'discipline' is now starting to fall apart. For many learning environments this may seem a step too far (for now) but Edison consciously created machine shops where a diverse range of skill sets worked in the same room. The advantages of multi-perspectives was not lost on 3M:

"Thomas Edison believed that a small group of people with varied backgrounds could be the most inventive. That's what I found when I joined (3M's) Central Research. I could talk to an analytical chemist, a physicist, people working in biology and organic chemistry – people in all the sciences. They were all within 50 yards."[3]

---

2 Wired Magazine, November 2012
3 Spencer Silver, in 'A Century of Innovation: The 3M Story, 2002, 3M

d) Learn by tinkering – MIT, Google and Edison Labs are all examples of 'inventing by doing'. In learning theory terms, this is a constructivist approach, where learning is built, layer upon layer, informed by the personal experiences/experiments of the learner. Contrast this with the 'company manual' approach where, for all but a few employees, learning is consumed, not constructed. Great machine-shop companies live and breathe tinkering philosophies. Edison maintained 'I have not failed. I've just found 10,000 ways that won't work.' Media Lab's early motto was a playful twist on the academic 'publish or perish': 'demo or die', meaning don't write up what it can do, show it.

2. **Keep It Social**

When Edison set up the organ for communal singing, or extended his prototype electric railway so it could take his workers fishing, or provided beer and food for all-night invention sessions, it wasn't very different to the free massages, laundry and food available at Valve. And it probably provided the inspiration for Mark Zuckerberg's pizza-fuelled, all-night 'hackathons' in the early days of Facebook.

As we see more widely now, the dividing line between work and play is often deliberately blurred in intensively creative workplaces. The remarkable thing about Menlo Park, however, is that the general public was encouraged to join the commons:

"The shops were places to socialise as well as work. Visitors were allowed easy access to the shops, whether they were men looking for work, boys looking for amusement, or amateur inventors looking for new ideas."[4]

---

[4] Millard, A. Machine Shop Culture and Menlo Park in *Working at Inventing: Thomas A. Edison & the Menlo Park Experience* (1989) Johns Hopkins University Press

We're increasingly seeing companies become social businesses – working with employees, partners, suppliers, and customers to 'maximise co-created value'. Scott Drummond is Social Media Director for HOST, one of Australia's leading advertising agencies. For him, helping companies develop a social media strategy is never really about the media:

> "It's the low-hanging fruit for organisations that have been used to talking at people. They say 'now we can talk at them through another channel'. But eventually they get past that and say 'oh, they're talking back!' For some people social media becomes a bridge to becoming a social business."

More and more business are coming to see that a business that's social, is not just a better way of connecting with customers, it's a route to better employee engagement. Scott Drummond again:

> "Switching social media on in a company is easy. Finding a way to legitimise it in a business context, to make people more capable, to incentivise them, to make them happier in their job – that should be a metric that we care about. Not just 'are we wringing an ounce more productivity out of them, but are they more engaged at work?'"

3. Make learning horizontally relevant

As we saw in the previous chapter, learning is most powerful when it is 'horizontally relevant'. In the Edison Labs every experiment, every 'learning moment' was trying to solve the problem immediately facing Edison and his muckers. Suppositions weren't filed away for later development. They were tested, however late the hour, there and then, in what Marcia Conner calls 'the moment of need':

"The Head of Human Resources in a large international company that I work with aims for learning agility throughout the organisation. He wants people to hear new ideas and put those into practice quickly and easily. Learning isn't just the taking in, but it's the application. It's thinking about how we're going to use what we're taking in and apply it in the moment of need, to what the business needs to be done."

4. Give learners the 'right-to-roam' on the commons

We saw, in Chapter Four, how games developer Valve insists that all employees choose the project they wish to work on, by following their passion. Google, 3M, and a host of other companies now offer 'free time' to employees. So, a true learning commons needs to give learners the right-to-roam, if only for some of their time.

At Menlo Park, the practice of moving between projects was known as 'tramping'. Workers were encouraged to work on a number of projects at once, rotating between them, when their expertise was needed, or when they thought they had something to offer. Critically, tramping doesn't just expand the learning of individual employees – it ensures that knowledge doesn't remain within silos, but circulates throughout the organisation.

5. From individual to collective, from formal to informal

By now, you'll have seen the emerging pattern: innovative companies create a learning environment that's fluid, collaborative, democratic, autonomous, and integrated into the work being done. This may not seem overly radical but it's a very long way from where most organisations currently sit.

For a start, many businesses still focus upon individual learning, but what we see in great learning organisations is a shift towards the collective knowledge of the company. Social

131

media has transformed the 'reach' of knowledge availability exponentially. This means that learning managers have quickly gone from 'how do I get the answer into your head?' to 'maybe the answer's in the room' to 'the answer's not even in the room, it's in the network'. Forget e-learning – the concept of Personal Learning Networks, facilitated through social media, is the biggest disruptive innovation to have hit workplace learning in 50 years.

Organisations, therefore, need to widen their focus. But company leaders who have not learned socially themselves, usually fail to appreciate the scale of the shift taking place. Indeed, Harold Jarche argues that, to understand it, you have to experience it:

> "Working and learning in networks is a fundamental shift from working and learning in a hierarchy or in the structured organisation, and the only way to really understand how different it is, is to engage it... You can't do a web-learning strategy for your organisation unless you're a web-learner; you don't realise what blogging does unless you've blogged; you don't know the power of Twitter, until you've used it."

Companies also need to see that, when it comes to work-based learning, they have been looking through the wrong end of the telescope. I highlighted the consensus earlier that about 90 percent of an employee's learning is informal – through experience, from mentors, or through their personal learning networks (which will reach beyond the company). The remaining 10 percent is gained through formal training. Why, then, do companies reverse these ratios when it comes to investing in learning? Ninety percent of company spend is on the formal, and only 10 percent on informal learning. That doesn't seem like a sensible use of money.

Here, however, is the paradox in going 'open': organisations are beginning to see that they need to become intentional about informal learning, and, in particular, social learning. A transition to more informal learning has to be managed, and they have learning officers to do just that. But, for informal learning to be effective, it depends on pull, not push. So leaders increasingly need to create the right growing conditions (culture and structure) sprinkle some seeds, and see what comes up, rather than imposing social learning on their businesses.

So Why Can't We All Be Like Edison?
Why Some Companies Learn and Others Fail

Successive studies highlight the main anxiety that keeps CEOs awake at night: adapting to change. One only has to look at the fortunes of Kodak – once the dominant business in personal photography, now declared bankrupt – to see the importance of creativity and agility. Innovation is pivotal to growth. Growth and innovation have been described as 'the inseparable twins of contemporary economics'. It's estimated that half of America's gross domestic product lies in intellectual property that for the sake of simplicity we'll define as the creation and exploitation of ideas.

Business Week's list of 2010's most innovative companies demonstrates a clear and consistent link between innovation and revenue growth: for proof, simply look at the performance of Apple, Google, Amazon, Nintendo and India's Reliance Industries (gas and oil production) – all in the top 20 companies for innovation and all enjoying revenue growth in recent years of at least 30 percent. So, why don't all companies take inspiration from the modern day inventions factories, some of which are featured here, and all of which are dominating their industries? What's stopping everyone from having their own Menlo Park? The simple answer is that, while every CEO wants their company to be innovative, there is less certainty in how to stimulate innovation and less still in how to build a vibrant learning culture.

It's now over 20 years since the publication of social scientist and management expert Peter Senge's seminal *'Fifth Discipline'* book, in which he persuasively argued that companies needed to become intentional about learning if they were to become successful organisations and fix the learning disabilities that led to organisational failure.

Despite widespread acknowledgement of Senge's case, we are, in many ways, not much further forward in our understanding of how companies can foster learning.

Corporate Learning's Identity Crisis

This vagueness is graphically illustrated in job titles given to people that I interviewed who have a responsibility for learning in companies – variously described as Chief Information Officers, Knowledge Managers, Learning & Development Officers, Training Officers, Directors of Learning & Collaboration, Learning Evangelists, even Catalyst for Magic (we'll meet her in a little while).

Despite learning's identity crisis, however, there are companies who see the need to create an innovative learning commons in their factories and offices. In order to do so they've pretty much abandoned everything they learned in business school (if indeed they ever went to one). In Part Two of this chapter we'll examine how they have done this, and hear from some of the leading learning professionals on the paradox entailed in managing a process by letting go of it.

For now, though, let's try to unpick the reasons why some companies succeed in creating learning commons while others can't or won't. Given that learning is an intensely personal process, it won't surprise you to learn that most of the blockers reflect people's personalities, insecurities and motivations.

Failure of Leadership

Though stating the obvious, it's nevertheless true that if a CEO is unconvinced about the need to create an innovative learning culture, it probably won't happen. Citing a study published in the British Journal of Management, Dan Pontefract, Head of Learning & Collaboration at Canadian telecoms giant Telus, writes: "leaders must not only make deep investment, they must scream from the hilltops that it's an important piece of organizational culture. Collaborative learning in a positive environment is critical to success."[5]

Recent research, however, would suggest that they not only have to believe in it – they have to live it, too. Hal Gregersen, Clayton Christensen and Jeff Dyer, in researching their book, 'The Innovator's DNA', found that CEOs at innovative companies spent twice as much time modelling innovation (asking questions, experimenting, connecting unconnected ideas) than those who led less innovative companies.

Take Garry Ridge, for example. Ridge is a typically outspoken Australian who moved to San Diego, eventually becoming the CEO of WD-40, the company whose mission is 'to create positive, lasting memories by stopping squeaks, getting rid of smells and getting rid of dirt'. WD-40 may not seem like a hot-bed of innovation but, in a fiercely competitive environment Ridge has more than doubled WD-40's turnover in his 12 years in charge. What's more, the $300m annual sales are achieved by only 300 employees – equivalent to $1m per employee.

---

[5] Garcia-Morales, et al, *The Effects of Transformational Leadership on Organizational performance through Knowledge and Innovation*, British Journal of Management December, 2008

In the early years of being CEO, Garry walked the talk, completing an executive leadership Masters programme at the University of San Diego (USD). The company now pays for other employees to complete advanced leadership programmes at USD. Ridge has also created a lunchroom library, where employees can borrow books on learning and leadership, and the 'Leadership Academy', where staff can discuss issues and listen to guest speakers on a wide range of interests – not all related to WD-40's core business.

Modelling the learning you wish to see in others is possibly the single most important thing that a CEO can do in creating a learning organisation. Sadly, too few CEOs are like Garry – for most, the personal learning journey ends once they've reached the head of the company.

Out-dated Organisational Structures, Cultures and Practices

Ridge inherited a learning culture, in which knowledge stayed in departmental silos:

> "So my biggest challenge was 'how do you turn silos of knowledge into fields of learning?' Why weren't people sharing? Well, they were scared out of their pants."

In order to get people to share freely Ridge had to remove the fear factor:

> "So, we don't make mistakes at WD-40 company. We have 'learning moments'. We had to start rewarding people for telling us that they'd screwed up. Not that they'd screwed up in a negative way, but that they'd screwed up in a positive way, and that they'd learned something from it."

Creating an innovative learning culture rarely produces a direct line between cause and effect. So learning managers are often under pressure to justify their existence through layers of evaluation. It also nudges learning back to the safe and predictable classroom-based models, because we all know how that works: present, test, forget - but at least we've got completed test papers.

Of course, e-learning was supposed to fix all that. But a lack of imagination in course design can't be rescued simply by being digitised. For too many e-learners (though please don't call them that), death-by-PowerPoint was replaced by death-by-clicking, and conversation was replaced by the multiple choice test.

The problem isn't the technology, it's the pedagogy (don't fret if this word is foreign to you, there's a passage coming up on the three ugliest words in the English language – pedagogy is one of them – but they're easily explained). Most formal training suffers from 'push' – what someone thinks you need to know to improve performance. By contrast, the learning which happens socially oozes 'pull' – which makes the training room seem like an even more alien place.

Mishandling Expertise, Creativity and Motivation

In most companies, therefore, learning still equates to training; expertise = content; creativity becomes a synonym for innovation, and motivation is found in a paycheque. Incidentally, if you're not sure of the difference between creativity and innovation, think of it this way: if you're the type of person who has lots of new ideas, you might be creative; you're only innovative, however, if you take some of those ideas and produce something with them.

Professor Teresa Amabile (whom we met in Chapter Five) has identified three core components of creativity: creative thinking skills, motivation, and expertise. She believes that managers can significantly influence each of these components, positively and negatively, through workplace practices and conditions. Though not directly part of her research, it goes without saying that work-based learning has a critical bearing on all three.

Amabile makes the important point that creativity killing practices are rarely the fault of a lone manager, but more often arise out of long-standing, usually unchallenged, systemic processes – how we do things around here. She points to a number of ways in which employees' expertise and creativity is blocked:

• Awarding false freedoms – giving employees apparent freedom to explore the means to a specified end, but in reality severely curtailing such freedoms, by proscribing the route, or frequently changing the destination.

• Cultivating a (inadvertent) culture of criticism – bosses usually don't set out to be negative towards new ideas. But Amabile's research suggests that '(other) people believe that they will appear smarter to their bosses if they are more critical - and it often works. In many organisations, it is professionally rewarding to react critically to new ideas'.

• Putting together homogenous teams – managers may look good if teams come to a solution quickly and without dissent. Job done. 'But homogenous teams do little to enhance expertise and creative thinking. Everybody comes to the table with a similar mindset. They leave with the same'.[6]

The cumulative effect of management mishandling, or micro-managing, creativity and expertise is that motivation drains away, and learning becomes a management-imposed chore, to be endured, rather than enjoyed.

---

[6] "How To Kill Creativity" Amabile, T. Harvard Business Review, October 1988

In order to better understand the difficulties corporations face in trying to foster collaborative, engaging, learning cultures, I met with Matt Moore, Knowledge Manager at Price Waterhouse Coopers, Australia, at the company's offices in Sydney's business district. Matt, a migrant Brit who doesn't look entirely comfortable in a suit, suggested we relocate to the nearest pub where, over a beer, he began by highlighting the tensions between personal development and motivation, and the need to build collaborative learning:

> "What gets badged as 'organisational learning' is really just the mass training of individuals. Corporations have to balance three levels of learning: the individual, the group and the corporate. When they get it wrong, it's usually the group that gets neglected."

Similarly, Matt believes that employee engagement programmes encourage individual advancement over collegiality. They usually offer rewards (salary increases, bonuses and non-monetary recognition) and participation (having a say in your workload, having input into company decision-making). Both are designed to bond the individual more closely to the company, but neglect the concept of the group. Moore also feels that employee engagement schemes fail to recognise the importance of intrinsic motivation as a key driver of engagement, and offer financial reward as a default, particularly if the company itself is driven by extrinsic factors (profits, sales).

Teresa Amabile reinforces Matt Moore's convictions: 'when people are intrinsically motivated, they engage in the work for the challenge and enjoyment of it... Managers in successful, creative organisations rarely (need to) offer specific extrinsic rewards for particular outcomes... The work itself is motivating... the most common extrinsic motivator managers use is money, which doesn't necessarily stop people from being creative. But, in many cases, it doesn't help either.'

In other words, companies can't mandate learning, because engagement – a pre-requisite of learning – can neither be bought, nor instilled. This, in part, explains the appalling inefficiency of most corporate training programmes. Remember Jay Cross's calculation that only 15 percent of what's learned in a formal setting is ever actually applied on the job? It's a safe bet that if you don't have the engagement of employees when you're teaching them, they're not likely to apply it in their work.

Part Two: Bringing the Commons to the SOFT Company

The changes we looked at in the preceding chapters – economic turbulence, the democratisation of knowledge, the shift from cultural consumption to production, the crisis of disengagement – all point to societal shifts, which can do no other than radically alter the world of work. The prolific growth of social movements in this century points to something more than passing unrest or dissatisfaction. Instead, we may be at the start of a new epoch, where we see the world, and how we should live our lives, as we've never seen before. Peter Senge eloquently sums it up:

> "At the deepest level, I think that we're witnessing the shift from one age to another. The most universal challenge that we face is the transition from seeing our human institutions as machines to seeing them as embodiments of nature... If you use a machine lens, you get leaders who are trying to drive change through formal change programs. If you use a living-systems lens, you get leaders who approach change

as if they were growing something, rather than just 'changing' something." [7]

Senge is saying that the era of top-down change, driven by a heroic-leader, is at an end; that if institutions and the people who work in them are to survive, then change needs to be cultivated, not driven. Senge argues that new growth comes through personal commitment, not compliance:

"I have never seen a successful organizational-learning program rolled out from the top. Not a single one. Conversely, every change process I've seen that was sustained and that has spread, started small. Usually these programs start with just one team... Deep change comes only through real personal growth – through learning and unlearning. This is the kind of generative work that most executives are precluded from doing by the mechanical mindset and by the cult of the hero-leader: The hero-leader is the one with 'the answers'."

In other words, we have to bring the Global Learning Commons into the company, and that means subscribing to the SOFT values and actions we identified in Chapter Three: Sharing, Open, Free, Trust. In the case studies that follow, someone, or some people, recognised the imperative to unlearn, and to shift hearts and minds away from closed to 'open' systems. All change starts with a value proposition and here are some to inspire.

---

[7] Peter Senge Interview with FastCompany magazine, April 1999

Sharing: Telus

Telus, the Canadian telecommunications company, has an explicitly stated, and award-winning, commitment to lifelong learning. In 2012 it made a learning investment of $23m for its 35,000 staff. It has won the BEST award (Building talent, Enterprise-wide, Supported by the organization's leaders, fostering a Thorough learning culture) from the American Society for Training and Development seven times, and enjoys very high employee engagement scores.

Collaboration and 'spirited teamwork' are one of their non-negotiable values: employees are known as team members. Their CEO, Darren Entwistle says, "You are successful when the appetite to learn is held as a responsibility shouldered by the entire management team and not by a functional remit within human resources."

Through Twitter, I met Telus's Senior Director for Learning and Collaboration, Dan Pontefract. High on his list of many achievements has been to shift from a model of learning, which was essentially didactic, to a blend of formal, informal (acquired on the job) and social (acquired, largely through social media). Underpinning this shift has been the Telus Leadership Philosophy, a model of simplicity, and therefore its power. The TLP has four jargon-free values: We embrace change and initiate opportunity; We have a passion for growth; We have the courage to innovate; We believe in spirited teamwork.

These values are delivered through a 'fair process' for all team members, who have an entitlement to: Engage; Explore; Explain; Execute; Evaluate

This process builds a collaborative culture through: Connected Learning; Leadership Framework; Social technologies.

And that's it. In honouring these values and processes however, a whole swathe of learning has happened, almost all

142

of it collaborative. Training courses in emotional intelligence, coaching and leadership skills, negotiating and presentation coaching, career development, and much more besides.

Dan also introduced a range of social media tools. Habitat Social is Telus's own collection of tools that emulate YouTube, Twitter, Facebook, SlideShare, Blogging, Wikis, Flickr and News aggregators. Repairmen and engineers in the field are able to upload videos of the problem facing them, and get a range of potential solutions in seconds.

A commitment to sharing radically alters the culture of organisations. Micro-blogging on Telus social media tools avoids departmental divisions, or water-cooler cliques. A new employee can be quickly plugged in to 'how-tos' and workarounds, hitherto only discovered through tacit learning, and potential costly errors can be averted, or nipped in the bud.

There's no doubt that social media is having a huge impact on sharing and collaboration. But I still maintain that it isn't driving it. What continues to drive it is the desire to meet with like-minded people, to connect ideas, and to take collaborative action, to achieve something that we couldn't achieve alone, and to feel good about it. Social media is actually facilitating more face-to-face sharing than ever before. It's not about the media, it's about the social.

Until the technology came along, collaboration like this couldn't have happened at scale, or at speed, but it's the social that gives 'pull' to the learning. Once companies fully embrace sharing, phrases like 'return on investment' become redundant. As Telus's Darren Entwistle said of Dan Pontefract "The reason it works is because he has created the pull. People see the business logic of it. They get the return on learning."

Open: Ingenious Media and AMP

Patrick McKenna is the CEO of Ingenious Media. Based in London, Ingenious Media is an investment and advisory group specialising in media, entertainment, sport, leisure and clean energy. They have advised some of the biggest names in the entertainment industry, including David Beckham, Robbie Williams, Channel Four, and invested in festivals, TV production companies and financially backed major films, including Avatar, the biggest grossing film of all time.

As a former Chairman of Andrew Lloyd-Webber's Really Useful Group, and one of the biggest media entrepreneurs in the world, Patrick appears, refreshingly, to play against type. He is a thoughtful, softly-spoken man who is as far removed from the image of a brash investor as possible. If he has an ego, (and it's hard to imagine someone who has made a fortune out of drama not having one) he keeps it well hidden.

I've known Patrick a long time and though he clearly knows a thing or two about money, it's been his involvement in education – he was a board member of The Liverpool Institute for Performing Arts when I was Director of Learning there – that allowed me to work with him. I was curious to see how the financial sector, famously discrete with its knowledge, was coping with a world gone SOFT, and coping with concepts like radical transparency. How for example did they deal with their biggest asset: intellectual property?

> "It's a bit like the open source software model. We give a lot of our knowledge away, so that people will engage us to deliver some implementation of that knowledge. We tell people everything we know. We don't have any great insights that we wouldn't want to share with everyone, because we're either raising investments, giving consultancy advice, or we are making investments. The

only way we can sell those insights is by sharing what we know. The reason why we don't worry about giving that knowledge away is because most people can't implement what they know. The capital value of something these days is the ability to implement it rather than to create it originally."

That's the business case for going 'open'. But there's another, more pragmatic reason. These days, it's almost impossible to keep a secret:

"Some of our original funds were marketed under confidentiality agreements, but the information still found its way out. Confidential information in the marketplace today, is tomorrow's reading for the rest of the world, so why bother trying to hide it? It's actually becoming much more open. We're the market leaders, so we have to take that approach – others have had to keep new funds that they're launching under the radar for as long as they can. When we first started we were a bit more circumspect about telling people what we were doing and why we were doing it. As time has gone on, we've learned to be much more transparent about our thinking."

Being more transparent means that their advisory activities are strengthened by their independence, and that their influence becomes greater:

"The music industry was the first to be hit by digital technology. It put its head in the sand and thought it would all just go away. They don't pick their heads up very often to view the landscape, so they needed to be reminded. As consultants to the music industry, we're not incumbents chasing sales and following repetitive old-fashioned practices. We act to provoke them into thinking what they ought to be doing next. Of course they (the music industry) all have their own strategy units, but they tend to be quite weak within the organisation. They're owned by the organisation, and are restricted in what they can say. Whereas independents, such as ourselves, can come in to look at future investment opportunities, and we can say where all this is heading."

Ingenious is a good example of 'inside-out' thinking to influence change. Advising and advocating change in an industry in which you have considerable investments makes sound business sense. A true learning commons, however, has no boundaries and learning also works 'outside-in'. Our next case study is a brilliant example of cultivating innovation by welcoming outsiders into the learning commons.

Amplifying Innovation

Let me introduce you to the aforementioned 'catalyst for magic', Annalie Killian. I met Annalie, almost by chance, at the end of a working trip to Australia. She kindly invited me to her house for dinner, so I interviewed her while she chopped food. With a job title like that, you might think that Annalie works for a whizzy, high-tech start-up. In fact, she works for AMP, the largest, and oldest financial services company in Australasia.

AMP deals in superannuation, pension plans, and life insurance – not the kind of company you expect to be at the cutting edge of collaboration tools. Companies like AMP have to have a brand that is seen as dependable, responsible and as reliable as the building they occupy (it's the iconic one which dominates Sydney's Circular Quay – you can't miss it). But they also have to be innovative. For Annalie Killian, creating a learning culture that supports innovation has been a slow process. Getting people to invest time and effort to seek out the technological and societal shifts, which have a significant bearing on AMP's future investments, hasn't been easy:

"I started working with innovation champions and said 'I'd like to take you with me so we can go and visit places. And you would think people would think 'well, it's a break from work'. But no, their comfort zone and the tyranny of the urgent would invariably win. So I said to my boss 'I want to bring ideas into the organisation so that people have to trip over them'. And she understood that there wasn't enough 'outside-in' thinking going on."

And so the Amplify festival was born. Amplify is unique – think TED talks[8] for accountants, and you wouldn't be far wrong (having spoken at one, it's a lot more fun than that sounds). Although Amplify posts its speakers' presentations online, its primary audience is AMP employees:

"In 2005, we ran the first Amplify festival of ideas over one day. In 2007, we did it over one week. Anyone in the company can attend, and we do it so they can plan their work around it. Amplify has a specific agenda: to look at technology as an indicator of social change. When technology changes, it changes the way human beings interact with each other. When that happens, business shifts. So we ask, 'what's happening at the edges and how might that change us five years from now?'"

Annalie's list of invited speakers for Amplify reflects her own unbounded curiosity. For 2013 (theme 'Shift Happened > Transformation Needed') Amplify's presenters included research

---

[8] www.ted.com

scientists, storytellers, data analysts, social innovators, submarine designers, film producers, social innovators – many financial institutions might question the value of bringing such a diverse range of thought leaders into their headquarters. But the return on investment is already apparent:

> "On the back of Amplify, we've managed to get very large investment in our data centre. And we've also had investments in bio-engineering, so it's affecting the direction of our current investments. We're now experimenting with business models. In a few years from now, for example, we think that 50% of work will be free-lance, so we're working with people to build co-creation spaces in which people rent time, rather than floor-space."

The lesson from both Ingenious Media and AMP is that 'open' demands a complete mind shift: from seeing internal knowledge as a property to be slavishly guarded and then exploited, to seeing it as a process, constantly being tested, augmented, challenged by visitors, and rethought, so that it creates a 'corporate mind', able to connect, imagine and innovate.

Free: 3M

3M make everything from skin care to car sealant, from touch screens to Scotch tape – 50,000 products, generating annual sales of more than $20bn. They're big. They got to be so big by having a 'tolerance for tinkerers' and, more importantly giving all staff time to tinker. Their '15 percent programme' was first implemented in 1948, and variants of it been adopted by many other companies since (including Google and Hewlett Packard). '15 percent time' has given birth to many of 3M's 22,000 patents. One of its most successful is worth detailing.

In 1968, Spencer Silver, one of 3M's corporate scientists, used the '15 percent programme' to come up with an adhesive that wouldn't leave any residue when removed. It was a novelty in search of a problem. Unfortunately, it didn't really work very well in its primary function: to hold things together. A glue that could come unstuck didn't seem like much of a proposition, and Spencer's colleagues found the whole venture rather amusing. Since the freedom to fail is built into 3M's DNA, Silver's innovation was put down to experience, and not taken into development.

Eight years later, another 3M scientist, Art Fry, was getting frustrated that the improvised bits of paper he was using as bookmarks in his church hymnal, kept falling out. *"If only there was a way to get bookmarks to stay in place,"* thought Art. Remembering Silver's failed attempt at non-residual glue, Art used his '15 percent time' to tinker with the consistency of Silver's adhesives, and thicknesses of paper so that it could become a repositionable bookmark.

But he still didn't know what use the product could be put to, and there wasn't much of a market for repositionable church hymnal bookmarks. It was only – so legend has it – when he had to take a phone message for a work colleague who wasn't at his desk, that he grabbed the paper, stuck the message on the desk, and the light bulb came on. What was originally called a 'Sticky Note', became the 'Post-It Note', and thanks to the freedom to fail and the use of 'free time' an industrial icon was launched.

Art Fry, however, is the first to admit that 3M needed an extraordinary collaborative learning culture to allow scientists to make the most of their '15 percent free time':

"I'd had 20 years of experience of developing new products prior to Post-It Notes. If I'd had the idea right out of college, I could never have made it a success, because

149

all of the chemistries and the processes involved were not something I learned in school – I had to learn them at 3M. At 3M we had the research people... out there on the fringes, bringing new materials out of the darkness. Then there are people like me who are in new product development who look at these things and say 'I wonder how they could solve problems?' We have an organisation called Technical Forum that shares technologies throughout the corporation. So, I was always going to seminars... to find out what was cooking."[9]

3M invests over $1bn a year in R&D, so 15 percent of that represents a substantial commitment. But all of 3M's employees are entitled to 15 percent time, not just the boffins,. This extraordinary employee entitlement marks the importance the company places on autonomy and the right-to-roam in the learning commons. The reward isn't simply a highly innovative culture, but loyalty, which measures careers at 3M in decades, and employee engagement stats which are off the charts.

But if simply giving employees 15 percent 'think-time' works, why hasn't it transformed the fortunes of those companies that have copied it? Well, it should be said that for at least one – Google – it has paid off, spectacularly. But Google, like 3M, put two other building blocks in place: a remarkable learning environment, and freedom to fail. For most of the copy-cats, the other two legs of the stool are missing.

At 3M, internal ideas can be taken externally and potentially bought back in, thus relieving pressure to 'repay' the company's generosity. But there is a tolerance for experiments that don't come off. And here's something to ponder: *over half* of 3M's inventions 'fail'. 3M has undoubtedly created a classic learning

---

[9] *A Century of Innovation: The 3M Story,* (2002), 3M

commons culture. One of the key success factors – and why others fail to copy them – is the capacity to share new ideas across 'open' structures.

Trust: IBM

Without trust as a core value, the other three values will never flourish. Building trust in an organisation is not simply the base that provides the safety net for innovative employees, it is repeatedly seen, in surveys, as the lead source of employee motivation. Remuneration, mistakenly considered the prime employee motivator, is only the sixth most important factor.

Most CEOs instinctively know this. Being able to turn this into 'doing' is another story. Many of the qualities that make CEOs dynamic change agents aren't conducive to trust-building. The stereotype of the decisive, macho leader isn't someone who favours listening, acknowledges mistakes, shares credit, or refuses to blame (remember the stat in Chapter Five that 37 percent of workers felt their boss had 'thrown them under the bus' to save themselves?). So, part of the reason for the knowing-doing gap is temperamental.

A bigger part, however, seems to be fear. If we allow staff to share, how can we rely on them to be responsible? How can we trust them to only use social media for work purposes? Or perhaps they fear what might happen if information is opened up. As Clay Shirky pointed out, one of the unknowns behind big data, is that you can't predict how people will use it:

"The thing that drives me craziest in conversations with large institutions about large data sets, is that they want to know, in advance, what will happen: 'why should we open up our data?', to which the answer is, you open up your data to see where the value is. It's the value you can't even predict until you try it, that you get back." [10]

Fear and trust are antithetical and it's fear, rather than trust, which is on the rise in the workplace. Bullying at work, for instance, has steadily risen during the past decade, to the point where, in 2010, 35 percent of all US employees claimed to have been bullied at work – that's over 50 million workers. [11]

Giving employees the freedom to fail, and to choose what, how and where they work would trigger anxiety attacks in many team leaders. But, as we have seen, the best 'learning moments' are in those moments of failure, and the most creative employees are found in situations where they have autonomy.

IBM was known for its closed-system operating systems, most notably the OS/2 platform. Such systems had provided the company with a huge market share of the business and personal computing industry. But with the open source software movement gaining ground, IBM was faced with a dilemma. To work with Linux and simply give away what they had hitherto made enormous profits from, was a high-risk strategy, and entirely dependent upon the community of developers making innovative use of their source codes.

Hindsight has shown that going 'open', and trusting their community was a commercial masterstroke, but it's only part of the story. IBM has truly become a Global Learning Commons in the past ten years. It was an early adopter of social media: its wiki central has hundreds of wikis, with hundreds of thousands of registered users; it hosts over 3,000 blogs and its own 'BlueTube'.

---

[10] Keynote speech at Educause Conference, 7th November 2011
[11] 2010 Zogby International poll commissioned by the Workplace Bullying Institute

Having held the same company values for almost 100 years, in 2003 IBM crowdsourced a new set of values, through a three-day 'Values Jam' on IBM's global intranet. (Remember this is the company whose lack of autonomy was typified through its employee acronym, 'I've Been Moved'.) The results were three values that now drive the company: Dedication to every client's success; Innovation that matters for the company and the world; Trust (that word again) and responsibility in all relationships

From being a company faced with a bleak future, IBM has transformed itself through learning commons principles. In 2012, it was recognised as first for leadership and fifth most admired company (Fortune magazine) and the eighteenth most innovative company in the world (FastCompany).

Corporate learning cultures cannot thrive unless fear is replaced by trust. No one can learn if they are fearful. Though first published 30 years ago, W. E. Deming's seminal '14 Points of Management' reminds us of the interconnection between trust and learning: 'Cease dependence on inspection to achieve quality... institute training on the job... break down barriers between departments... institute a vigorous programme of education and self-improvement... drive out fear, so that everyone may work effectively for the company'. [12]

Despite a million company change programmes and a plethora of management theories it's remarkable how little progress has been made. As Marcia Conner observed, 'W. Edwards Deming encouraged management to drive out fear and break down barriers between departments, and still worry and walls are the two constants that most organisations share'. [13]

---

[12] Deming, W. E. *Out Of The Crisis,* (1982), MIT Ctr for Advanced Educational Services
[13] *Where Social Learning Thrives,* FastCompany Magazine February 2011

It's often said that control-and-command management is (or should be) dead in today's work environment. The lesson to be learned from IBM is that trust demands courage; the courage to let go, the courage to trust others, and, more than anything, the courage to jump the knowing-doing gap.

*****

All of the case studies I've shared are proof that bringing the commons to the SOFT company not only makes for an innovative learning culture, but it makes business sense too. But there's another more compelling reason to change, and it's this. These values and actions – Share, Open, Free, Trust – are looked for and displayed every day that we interact socially, outside the workplace.

We, as citizens and customers, now expect these behaviours to be modelled by organisations, just as much as we expect to see them being socially responsible and green. If we don't see the values and actions that we display to each other elsewhere in business, we'll simply take our business elsewhere.

Revolutions happen in the space between an old system breaking down, and a new one becoming established. The old system of work-based learning was designed for the industrial age, but the 'open revolution' has not yet shaped the learning system we'll need for future needs. There is, however, no point in waiting until it all settles down.

As Clay Shirky argues, whatever embarrassment organisations feel when they go 'open' is more than off-set by the improvements they make as a result:

"Open systems always look completely terrible and shoddy when we first look at them, because we're used to institutions that hide all of their failures. But it's actually institutions that expose what it is they're doing to public criticism that improve the fastest."

Arie De Geus, Head of Shell's Strategic Planning Group, once famously said that 'the ability to learn faster than your competitors may be the only sustainable competitive advantage'. Like Thomas Edison's invention factory, Google's capacity to fail fast and iterate, is what has not only given them a competitive advantage, it has also made them the most desirable company in the world to work for. There's a good reason why Googlers at the Mountain View HQ describe it as 'the campus'.

What we've seen, from Menlo Park to Mountain View, is that the most innovative companies in the world regard work as learning. And what we're about to see is that the world's most innovative schools present learning as work.

Chapter Eight

Open Learning in Education

There's a widely-used activity favoured by consultants whenever educators are taking part in training programmes. It's called 'Significant Learning Experience' and it usually goes like this:

1. In groups, discuss the most significant learning experience you can recall from your youth – this may have taken place in formal education (school/college) or informally.

2. Try to identify any common characteristics of that experience.

3. Discuss how often those characteristics are present in the learning you lead at your school/college.

I'd invite you to do this exercise yourself, now. Just put the book down and cast your mind back to something that had a profound impact upon you, changing what you thought you knew, or thought you could do. Think about who else was involved, what circumstances lay behind it, and the context in which the learning took place. As you're probably reading this book alone, ask someone nearby to do the same thing (don't worry, they won't mind – people love talking about their learning). See if there are any commonalities. Come back to me when you've done parts 1 & 2...

I've lost count of the number of times I've done this exercise with people and heard the same conversations, seen the same scribblings on post-it notes. What follows are typically the key points to emerge, and I'd invite you to see how many of these accord with your own memories.

Most of the powerful learning experiences happened outside school or college (e.g. learning to swim, ride a bike, process life-changing events). They involve some kind of mentoring, backed up by some form of study group. They arise from some form of project – putting on a play, realising an ambition – that blends thinking and doing. They involve challenge, risk, and learning from failure. They force us to put ourselves outside our comfort zone, working through our doubts and fears, often by trial-and-error. There's invariably that light-bulb moment, followed by a gain in confidence and pride. People frequently recall some form of public presentation helping to cement the experience in our memories.

There's often an uncomfortable silence and much looking at shoes when I ask them to share how often they see these characteristics in the learning activities they lead. I make a point of doing this exercise as respectfully as I can because, firstly, I'm not the one who's in a classroom trying to coax learning out of a reluctant bunch of 14-year-olds on a wet Thursday afternoon; and secondly, because the aforementioned loss of autonomy has affected educators as much as it has call centre operatives. Their freedom to inspire learners has been curtailed by increasing prescription from above. But I also have to remind them that, having done this exercise with thousands of educators, I've yet to meet one that had their most significant learning experience from completing a worksheet.

Occasionally, I'll get asked for my most significant learning experience, and I'll share it here by way of introducing a chapter which, after looking at the many challenges facing education, shares some of the secrets of great learning institutions, and the traits of their learning leaders.

I was around 13 years old when my cousin, Alan Price, visited us at my parents' house. He had recently left a pop group called The Animals, at the peak of their success (their biggest hit, House of The Rising Sun, reached No 1 in both UK and US charts), and was recuperating from exhaustion back in the north-east of England. Naturally, as a kid who was learning to play the piano, Alan was something of a hero to me. My mother was quick to push me on the piano, to stumble through my most recent attempts to read music. It was terrible. Alan, however, was suitably supportive, but then asked a question I had never even considered: "It's good, David, but did you ever think about playing music without the notes?"

Of course I hadn't. Every piano teacher I'd been to, and every music lesson at school, reinforced the idea that music was read first, and then played. Alan, however, had never learned to read music, so, for a couple of hours he proceeded to show me how to play by ear. It's fair to say that those couple of hours of informal learning changed the course of my life.

From then on, I used to borrow all of my sister's records, work out the chords by ear, and by the evening I could be playing them on the beat-up old piano in my local youth club. Girls began to acknowledge my existence. I had, to quote Sir Ken Robinson, found 'my element'.

This immediate, trial-and-error, hands-on, project-based form of learning needed to be reinforced and stretched by a study group. Except we called it a band. We organised our own gigs, argued over song arrangements, harangued people to come watch us play and, inevitably, embarrassed ourselves in front of our peers. But, at the age of 15, we thought we were the coolest guys in the whole of Hebburn – maybe even Jarrow, too. And I got my first girlfriend. I might have been a little smug at that time, I can't remember.

Meanwhile, back in the learning enclosure, I was being lectured about the lives of dead white guys like Bach and Mozart and singing traditional English folk songs like the 'Miller of Dee'. That we would be remotely interested in the life of a selfish, alcoholic miller in the 18th century ("I care for nobody, no, not I, if nobody cares for me.") never seemed to occur to my school music teacher. She knew nothing of my extra-curricular music activities, and that was fine by me, because I had decided, a long time ago that I would drop music as an academic subject as soon as I could and before I died of boredom.

I hasten to add that I had nothing against 'old' music. When I was about 14 years old, I remember watching someone I later discovered to be Leonard Bernstein conducting Stravinsky's 'Rite of Spring', and bursting into tears at the passion, complexity and visceral audacity of the sounds I was hearing. We just weren't getting any of that blood, guts and sweat in the music classroom. Too busy singing about arrogant millers in bloody Chester...

I was lucky, therefore, to have a pop-star relative to impart my most significant learning experience, but it still carried all of the characteristics mentioned earlier: out of school, confidence-building, involving a mentor, challenging, practical.

As I realised later in life, people have been learning to play music informally, practically and successfully since Adam sang to Eve, and yet it wasn't until 2002 that the first significant study of those informal learning processes appeared, when Lucy Green, a Professor at the Institute of Education in London published, 'How Popular Musicians Learn: A Way Ahead for Music Education'. Until then, nothing.

The Power of the Informal

Shaped by these formative experiences, almost all of my work in learning has been to look outside-in, to see how the ways in which we learn socially and informally can be brought into more formal learning environments, in order to spark the kind of passion for learning that most of us experience in the social space.

I was lucky, in that my significant learning experience was really significant. I was able to make a career out of music, so it changed the shape of my life. Though not always of this magnitude, most people's significant learning experiences are usually of the informal variety. So why is there such reluctance to acknowledge the power and processes of informal learning?

We have come to accept that the most effective form of learning comes from the top-downwards, embodied in logic and deductive reasoning, with little room for intuition, abstraction, and tangential thinking. And, of course, for many learners and learning challenges, these formal methodologies work well. But not always.

Ricardo Semler, author of 'The Seven Day Weekend', recounts a meeting with a planning director of a major oil company. Charged with the job of predicting the future price of a barrel of oil, he explained the complex calculations, factoring in geo-political criteria, geological surveys and the chances of war, that were just some of the variables his team of 110 people took into account.

And after all the number crunching, their prediction turned out to be more than double the actual price of a barrel of oil. The oil executive's hunch, on the other hand, had the price of a barrel of oil to within a few dollars of the actual price. Ricardo couldn't resist:

"Why couldn't he rely on the intuition bolstered by his experience in the oil industry? He cocked his head like a mystified poodle and said 'imagine me telling a board that I've been sitting by the pool, debating with my dog, and concluding that oil will be $23 dollars in five years time?'"

But why are you still in your job, I asked, if your official forecasts are so off the mark?

"Ah said the man... I have the right to be wrong, but only so long as I am precisely wrong!"[1]

I am not suggesting here that gut instincts are superior to logic, evidence gathering and rationality. Simply that some rebalancing would be advisable.

I had this vividly brought home to me when I worked with Sir Paul McCartney in helping to set up The Liverpool Institute for Performing Arts, a tertiary college, which opened in 1996. Being the lead patron, and a significant funder, Paul took a keen interest in the college's early development. One day I met with him to look over the curriculum we'd designed and to discuss how he might play a part through occasionally teaching there.

It's not every day that a business meeting starts with an ex-Beatle doing an Elvis Presley impersonation while playing the *actual* double-bass which was used on 'Heartbreak Hotel' (I admit it, I was impressed). He was, however, less confident when it came to what he might teach:

"I suppose I could show them how I write songs (thoughtful pause)... but, actually, I don't know how I'd do

---

[1] Semler, R. *The Seven Day Weekend: A Better Way to Work in the 21st Century* (2004) Arrow Books.

that, because I don't know how I write, and I've never really analysed it, in case it disappears."

Sir Paul never learned how to read music, and never went to university. Recognising a working-class 'impostor syndrome' at work, I suggested to him that he did have a technique, he may just not have been conscious of it. The story of how McCartney came to write 'Yesterday' – by waking with the song fully formed in his head – is part of pop music mythology. Except it isn't true.

Yes, the tune was pretty much all there, but the words weren't. In the days that followed, Paul was to be heard singing *'Scrambled eggs, all I really want is scrambled eggs...'* As I explained to him, this frequently adopted technique is known as a 'dummy lyric' – a piece of nonsense to hang the melody on, so that constant repetition can suggest more meaningful lyrics that scan, rhyme, and make more sense.

It was at this point in the conversation that I heard a voice in my head saying, 'you really think it's a good idea to tell the world's most successful composer how he writes songs, do you?' Fortunately, Paul took no offence and still regularly teaches at the Institute. His mantra, 'trust your instincts' is as applicable to students as it is to him.

We may not yet understand the neuroscience behind instinctual decision-making which informs oil executives and creative artists alike, but that's because, until recently, we didn't value it.

'Hacking' Education

For 150 years, formal education has adopted an 'inside-out' mindset – schools and colleges have usually been organised around the needs of the educators, not the learners. In areas such as research, this is nothing to be embarrassed about.

Ground-breaking inventions and pioneering new thinking often arise from the selfishness that informs so-called 'blue-sky' research. Defending such freedoms from the external drive for practical and commercial implementation has often encouraged a necessary insularity.

The new landscape presents a significant upheaval. Inventors and researchers are increasingly working independently outside academia, finding collegial collaboration in the Global Learning Commons. Learners also find themselves in the driving seat because formal education is no longer the only game in town for those eager to learn. How colleges and universities adapt to the customisation and personalisation of education will largely determine their survival. Let me explain.

The challenge presented by Massive Open Online Courses (MOOCs) is a high-profile example, but not the only one, of a desire for us to 'hack' our own learning. The development of MOOCs has been likened to the creation of online music stores. The emergence of the mp3 allowed listeners to assemble their own playlists of music.

Whether paying for it, or pirating it, suddenly, they didn't have to buy a whole CD to get to the one song they really liked – they began to 'hack' their music listening. And we all know what a cataclysmic event that was for the music industry. It has to be conceded that they did themselves no favours by persecuting 13-year-olds, when they should have been rethinking their business models to reflect consumer preferences.

Similarly, educational institutions have to grasp that having enjoyed an historic monopoly as the go-to-guys for learning doesn't mean they always will. As we gained control of our listening with the arrival of the mp3, so we will increasingly gain control of our learning, thanks to the arrival of MOOCS, social media and informal learning. We will want to determine whom we learn from, and with whom, at a time of our pleasing.

Although this upheaval is currently taking place in tertiary education, schools are far from safe. As we find ourselves increasingly able to 'hack' our own education, I would expect, for instance, the homeschool market to expand rapidly. Once the possibility exists for students to study informally, at online (and offline) schools, compiling their own learning playlist, putting together units of study that appeal to their passions, the one-size-fits-all model of high school will appear alarmingly anachronistic. So, if educators want to keep their students engaged and inside their buildings, they have to look at the way they learn outside, and bring those characteristics inside.

Schools In Search Of A Purpose

If schools are coming into direct competition with the learning opportunities available in the informal social space, it has to be said that this is a pressure, which barely registers within the political discourse. Indeed, the gaping hole in the middle of the public debate on schooling is that we can't even agree on what schools are actually for. Do they provide a set of skilled employees for the labour market? Or are they about developing the 'whole' child – emotionally, intellectually, creatively? Do they serve to ensure national economic competitiveness? Or are they about civic cohesion through cultural education? These are questions around which there has been no public consensus, as absurd as this may seem, given that in the US and most of Europe we have had state-organised systems of compulsory schooling for over 140 years.

This failure to define a clear purpose has fatally held back progress in understanding how we learn best. For if you can't agree on a destination, how can you possibly agree on the best route? Instead, what we're left with is a public discourse permanently afflicted by the curse of binary, oppositional arguments.

The either/or positioning isn't helped by constant political interference, resulting in a series of pendulum swings with every change of administration. Polarised arguments prevent real progress being made: selective vs comprehensive school systems; instruction-led teaching vs inquiry-led; head vs hand; academic vs vocational; knowledge vs skills. Can you imagine doctors in the 21st century arguing over the use of flu vaccines?

With No Particular Place To Go

It goes without saying that, if we don't know our destination, and therefore can't agree on the best route to get there, we might struggle to measure distance travelled. When I look at the radically differing educational strategies currently being adopted by most developed countries, I think back to how I learned to drive a car. Please allow this diversion. It has a point.

It was the late 1970s, in the Republic of Ireland, at a time when, inexplicably, learner drivers were allowed to drive unaccompanied. Working in County Clare, in the south-west of the country, my employer let me drive his car so I could prepare for my driving test on my return to England. One day, I was driving down winding country roads, and realised I was hopelessly lost - anyone who has experienced Irish road signs will know this is easily done. Stopping a passing farmer, I asked if I was on the road to Kilrush, my destination. The farmer paused for some considerable time, looked up the road, then down at me, and pronounced *"You are, but your car's pointing the wrong way..."*

So it is with educational policy. When the political pendulum swings in western nations, getting 'back to basics' in education (shorthand for focusing upon literacy and numeracy) becomes an easy exhortation. If confirmation is needed that 'progressive' methods have failed, one only has to cite steadily declining performances in international comparison tables like the Programme for International Student Assessment (PISA). This decline is then contrasted with nations like Singapore and South Korea, who excel in these assessments.

What is being measured is entirely dependent upon the intended destination. While the UK and US urge their schools to be more like those of Pacific Asian countries, the pressure there is to travel in the opposite direction. Addressing teachers in 2012, Heng Swee Keat, Singapore's Minister for Education, argued for a radical shift in policy:

> "The educational paradigm of our parents' generation, which emphasised the transmission of knowledge, is quickly being overtaken by a very different paradigm. This new concept of educational success focuses on the nurturing of key skills and competencies such as the ability to seek, to curate and to synthesize information; to create and innovate; to work in diverse cross-cultural teams; as well as to appreciate global issues within the local context."[2]

These comments came shortly after South Korea's ex-minister for education Byong Man Ahn cast doubt on the usefulness of a high PISA ranking, despite Korean students ranking first in reading and maths, and third in science, in the 2009 PISA survey:

> "While Korea's students excel at learning, they believe its purpose lies not in self-development based on personal interest or motivation, but in entrance into a highly ranked university. Students have no time to ponder the fundamental question of "What do I need to learn, and why?" They simply need to prepare for the test by learning

---

[2] Address to 6th Teachers Convention in Singapore 31st May 2012

the most-effective methods for digesting tremendous quantities of material and committing more to memory than others do."

Both Heng Swee Keat and Byong Man Ahn were, effectively, repeating the advice given to me by that Irish farmer. Their respective countries had travelled a long way, but they'd realised that their car was pointing the wrong way.

We in the West want to be more like those in the East, who, in turn, want to be more like we in the West. We call for learning fit to meet the challenges of the 21st century, while recommending teaching methods belonging to the 19th century. We have no clearly agreed purpose for education, but agree that spurious international comparisons should inform future educational policy. In short, we're really, really confused.

The Pioneer Mavericks

You may have gathered by now, that, in general, we shouldn't look to our policy makers and politicians for either insight or inspiration when trying to imagine future learning. We could, however, make an exception for the aforementioned Heng Swee Keat. In the teacher's address mentioned earlier, he identified five traits of the 21st-century teacher:

1. Ethical Educator – a role model to students demonstrating integrity and moral courage.

2. Competent professional – continually developing new knowledge, skills and dispositions to lead.

3. Collaborative learner – engaging in professional conversations, enhancing the teaching fraternity.

4. Transformational leader – inspires colleagues to reflect and innovate, builds trust, manages change.

5. Community builder – understands local and global issues, developing students' sense of social responsibility.

If you don't spend much time in schools, these traits might not seem particularly radical. Trust me on this one – they are. Most teachers in an average high school would struggle to see themselves in those capacities – not because they don't want to be that kind of teacher, but because the system neither values nor cares about those traits.

There are, however, educators who not only demonstrate the traits of 21st-century teachers and leaders, but have also reconfigured learning in their institutions so that they are becoming true Global Learning Commons. In researching this book, I visited some of them, watched how learning happens under their leadership, and asked them to share their innovations and aspirations. To a greater or lesser extent, they are mavericks – in education systems that make a virtue out of compliance and conformity; it's almost inevitable that innovators will be seen as such.

School of Communication Arts 2.0, London

The School of Communication Arts 2.0 is tucked away on a rundown housing estate in Vauxhall, London. There are no smart reception areas, no glass atriums – there isn't even a sign above the door. This is intentional because each year each new cohort of students takes the shell of the building and fashions their own learning environment out of it, from scratch. It's a tertiary level school, but offers no qualifications and has no university affiliations. Despite an unprepossessing fabric the school promotes itself as 'the best advertising school in the world' – and it probably is.

The school is led by Marc Lewis. If Marc were ever going to head up a tertiary organisation, it would have to be one he created himself. He has no degree. In fact he has virtually no high school qualifications either, having been expelled from school at the age of 16. Not that a lack of qualifications has held him back. After building a chain of comedy clubs in South Africa, he returned to England to develop an internet start-up in 1997. Three years later, he sold it for just under £20m.

Although Marc established a reputation for digital mobile technologies, his training was in advertising. He gained a scholarship at what was the original School of Communication Arts, headed up by the man who became Marc's mentor, John Gillard. The 1.0 version closed in 1995, when John became too ill to continue. In 2010, Marc was able to relaunch the school, based on a highly innovative design:

"I was in Boston when I had the Eureka moment. I had a technology business that was selling to retailers, and I was in a drug store head office in Boston. They had all these plasma screens, on which were lists of schools together with who, in the head office, was mentoring in these schools. The US has a culture for mentoring, for transferring knowledge from A to B as directly as possible. And that's not in our culture in the UK. So I had a Damascus moment, I guess."

The school is built around a model of 'Heroes and Legends'. The two legends are industry giants, Bartle, Bogle and Hegarty, and Abbott, Mead, Vickers. Together, they offer the school sponsorship and industry credibility. A larger group of Heroes also offer money and their time and expertise. Combined, this financial support enables half of the school's students to receive a scholarship, and buys a stake in an investment fund, which supports graduate start-ups. 600 mentors provide masterclasses, guidance and briefs for students to work on. This unique model also provides for easy access to industry employment for students – most are snapped up by mentors.

All of this creates a blurring of the boundaries between study and work, but it's SCA 2.0's approach to learning that is perhaps the most radical. It is an approach that brings together three of the four values/actions of the Global Learning Commons: share, open and free.

Marc's design for SCA 2.0 was in response to the dilemma facing all universities – how to stay relevant, given the arcane approval processes which governs course creation and modification:

> "The university system is built on an industrial age economy, where knowledge evolves very slowly. In an information age economy, knowledge moves very quickly and areas of specialism are discovered more rapidly. If you're joining a course today, you're taking a programme that was probably written five to ten years ago, so a lot of that knowledge is out of date, irrelevant."

SCA's solution is an open source 'curriculum wiki'. Anyone – heroes, legends, mentors or students – can propose, design, or amend a course unit. They are also invited to contribute resources: stories, articles, books, videos. These are all made public on the SCA 2.0 website:

> "Once a year I pause curriculum wiki. I write it in educational language – learning aims and outcomes – and I write a delivery plan. Mentors are all around the world

and may, or may not have a hand in teaching, but they do have a point of view about what should be taught. Students share in curating the curriculum wiki with the industry. As stuff gets uploaded, it gets tweeted, so anyone in the world can consume this knowledge. Every day Saatchi & Saatchi or Ogilvy can go on to the wiki, and define what the next group of students need to be learning. So our curriculum is always in flux, always changing."

Because of this collaborative hacking, mentors and students can see that the course is both current, and relevant to the needs of the communications industry. While a unit or project brief is in progress, students are required to share their reflections publicly, through blogs and other social media. And the extensive use of social media not only makes the learning public, it serves as a marketing tool for SCA 2.0. In 2012, they received 2,000 applications for the 36 highly-sought-after places.

Students are expected to work on about 50 briefs during their course of study. These, according to Marc, fall into three categories: "Live (competitive and remunerated) briefs are about learning how to sell your work to a client, and earning some reputation; portfolio briefs are about showing how revolutionary your thinking is." The other briefs are akin to Facebook 'hackathons': 24-hr intensive challenges, that enable students to experience working under pressure. The quality, and ingenuity, of student responses to the briefs is astonishing. If you need proof, visit the school's homepage: it's impossible to tell which campaigns are real and which are simulations.

The near-guarantee of a job at the end of their study, or seed funding for a new business seems to more than compensate students for not having a degree to show for their work. In keeping with some of the other schools featured here, there is a common implication: as the link between having a degree and

171

guaranteed employment weakens, cultivating entrepreneurial, creative and collaborative skills in students will become paramount.

Marc is convinced of the transferability of a model of open-sourced curriculum and mentor-led delivery, and plans to set up similar schools in other sectors: "My belief is that university is the wrong place to teach vocations, period. The system is broken and if we can demonstrate the relationship between the industry, learner, and place of learning, then we can take it into other domains."

Sydney Centre for Innovation in Learning (SCIL)

You wouldn't typically expect to see a hothouse of educational innovation in a quiet, middle class, leafy suburb of Sydney. But that's exactly where you'll find the Sydney Centre for Innovation in Learning. Located on the edge of bushland in the city's Northern Beaches district, SCIL is perhaps what would have happened had Thomas Edison been an educator, rather than an inventor. A classic commons environment, it serves to ensure that ideas are 'free-range', brought into the commons from anywhere in the world, shared and tested among innovative practitioners, and then sent back out again.

SCIL is located within Northern Beaches Christian School (NBCS), whose principal is Stephen Harris. Stephen is a deceptively modest and quietly-spoken leader harbouring big visions and ambitions. In talking to Stephen, you get an overwhelming sense of a restless mind. He seems to find inspiration for new ways of designing learning everywhere he looks. A beautifully-designed airport terminal? That's how a school's central area could look, with students choosing their destination for today's learning. On a visit to the UK, I once took him to a pub in Hull on a cold, wet, windy, late summer's day. By the time we'd passed through an historic English urban landscape – Hull's deserted Museum Quarter – Stephen had redesigned it as an engaging set of learning locations.

He took over NBCS as a struggling k-12 school in 1999 and engineered its transformation through a culture of sharing, openness and, crucially, trust. Understanding that teachers would need a safe space in order to model much-needed, new teaching approaches, SCIL was originally envisaged as an internal professional development initiative, led by Anne Knock. Anne, a pragmatic completer-finisher, is a perfect foil to Stephen's 10-ideas-before-breakfast. She summarises SCIL's three areas of interest as 'people, places and pedagogy' and all three impact upon each other.

Believing that 'you can't teach new skills in old boxes', Anne and Stephen have systematically set out a programme of radical transparency, destroying learning enclosures by knocking down walls, and building new, large, airy spaces that look more like Googleplex than a conventional school.

For Stephen, this radical opening of space (classes are frequently held for 180 students at a time) fosters a 'de-privatisation' of teachers' domains and work practices (six teachers need to work as a team with those 180 students).

Management consultant Peter Drucker famously said that 'culture eats strategy for breakfast' and school cultures can be notoriously resistant to change, so getting teachers at NBCS to abandon their desks and behind-closed-door practices could not have been easy. By encouraging teachers to work in teams, in classes with mixed-age groups, with a greater emphasis on students following group inquiries, rather than filling in worksheets, Stephen claims that cultural shift became inevitable:

"If teachers were doing an MBA, they'd get pushed into collaborative teams. But no university, no courses are teaching our teachers to do that. Once they recognise the pressures that come off them as a result of working in collaborative teams, they very rarely want to go back."

Stephen, Anne, and other teachers at NBCS, travelled the world in search of innovation. As a result, the pace of change quickened and staff began to see themselves as professional researchers as much as teachers. As word spread that something different was happening at NBCS, Anne's role became more outward facing:

> "My job is now with the educational community outside our school gate. The chance to play a part in influencing education more broadly is very exciting. When people come here they come because they think they're seeing buildings... and then they talk with random students and teachers, and say 'I thought I was coming here to see a building. Now I know it's so much more'."

In today's culture of high-stakes accountability, freedom to innovate is only tolerated if student outcomes improve. NBCS can point to improved results, year-upon-year, at all levels throughout the school since the transformation began. But how were parents persuaded to be part of the change process? And how did new students take to a school with significantly greater freedom given to students, but significantly greater responsibility expected of them?

Crucially, that's where trust comes in. Parents need to be willing to trust SCIL's judgment on which innovations to adopt, and which to reject. Teachers need to trust their students, and everyone needs to trust the process, even if things appear to get worse before they get better. Losing faith in the process, according to Anne, is one of the reasons that innovations get abandoned too soon:

"Ultimately the parents are trusting what we're doing, and we've got to respect that trust. From a teacher perspective, those first few weeks are terrible, just helping kids to get into that different way of thinking and behaving. Then the kids get it, and they settle. But sometimes people try to change, get frightened, and then they stop too soon."

Stephen's visionary leadership has created the context and culture for innovation to flourish. After that, he simply trusts teachers to use their professional judgments in order to realise what he calls 'multimodal' learning:

"We're living in a world where one laptop per child doesn't capture it. They're using three or four devices (mobile, laptop, iPod, etc.). Students need to be able to switch seamlessly between online learning and face-to-face, and teachers need to deploy multiple forms of input. I'd want to influence teachers to realise that the more students own their learning, the quicker the journey will be. But I'm not about to tell teachers how to do that."

SCIL offers a provocation to the concept of the compliant teacher, passively implementing learning designs created by others. Through SCIL, a profound culture shift has taken place in NBCS. Teachers have become designers of learning, and of the spaces in which learning happens. Innovation now drives the learning. It has taken a nascent learning commons culture and made it global:

"SCIL started off as an activity within the school. We're now thinking of reversing that, so that SCIL is the body, of which Northern Beaches is the flagship school. That then frees us up to start growing new ideas of what school might look like. That might be a school for adolescents that runs from 4.00 p.m. to 9.00 p.m. to match their circadian rhythms. It could be an inner-city warehouse school; it could be a school in Rwanda or Cambodia. Eventually, the idea of 'school' is going to transform to become, at heart, a functional community, that becomes a base station for kids as they launch into life."

High Tech High Schools, San Diego County, USA

The final of our three case studies is a group of schools in and around San Diego. They span elementary, middle and high schools, each containing a maximum of about 450 students. Their founder and CEO is Larry Rosenstock – an ex-carpenter-cum-attorney from America's east coast, who moved to Southern California to run the Price Charitable Fund. Having previously worked in very traditional high schools in Cambridge, Massachusetts, Larry had a good idea of what he felt didn't work with urban high schools. So when the chance came to set up a small school in San Diego, he jumped at it.

Larry is a leader who preaches what he practises: he developed a sharp analytical mind through his legal training, but his first love is working with wood. This love is apparent from a visit to his house in La Jolla, just outside San Diego. He showed me the cabin he built himself out of redwood and cedar. It's a thing of beauty, entirely fashioned to host a small window, originally owned by Frank Lloyd Wright, found in a junk shop many years ago.

Larry is a living embodiment of the MIT motto, *mens et manus*: mind and hand. He leads by example: at High Tech High you will never find a separation of students based on academic ability and (further down the pecking order) those deemed 'good with their hands'. Both skills are seen as important, both are nurtured.

As soon as the first school filled up, the school's board approved another. And another. Having opened the first High Tech High school in 2000, they have averaged one new school a year. School graduation rates are 100 percent. Almost 100 percent of students go to college, with an average of 80 percent completing four-year university programmes. 35 percent of their students are the first in the family to go to college.

All of these stats are impressive of course, but to really grasp why High Tech High differs from most schools, you have to see it for yourself. I've visited on numerous occasions and I've yet to walk around one of the schools without a student asking to show me his, or her, work. If you ever visit schools, you'll know how unusual this is. And work is the operative word here. There are few conventional classrooms, rather they have workshops or studios. Student work is on display everywhere you look, largely because High Tech High's main vehicle for learning is 'the project'.

High Tech High is probably one of the world's leading exponents of project-based learning (PBL). If you're unfamiliar with PBL, it's frequently (and usually wrongly) associated with a generalised approach to learning by 'topics', which was popularised in the 1970s and vilified thereafter for its laissez-faire, anything-goes, laxity. In the hands of expert practitioners, like those at High Tech High, PBL is what most of us do for a living: we have a need, a client, some complex questions to answer, and we come up with a collaborative solution – all within a timeframe.

The student projects at High Tech High are usually located 'out there' in the community: The Blood Bank Project for the San Diego Blood Bank to raise awareness of the need to donate blood; students developed a DNA bar-coding system for identifying illegally-traded meat from protected animals in Tanzania; The San Diego Bay Study has been a 10-year project which produced books (with forewords written by conservationist Jane Goodall); built gardens; produced original research findings... you get the idea. The shorthand term for PBL is 'learning by doing' but, in the right hands, it's much more than that.

It's clear that judged by their exam results, High Tech High students produce the required outcomes. But the depth of their knowledge – and their capacity (as Professor Guy Claxton puts it) 'to know what to do, when you don't know what to do' are the main reasons why so many get accepted onto university programmes. At High Tech High, the learning is found in the work that students do, and it's work that matters.

By now, it should come as no surprise to see that student engagement doesn't come at the expense of high-performance, but rather is a precursor to it. The Holy Grail – in business or in education – is creating the environment and the organisational structures that secure engagement. My view is that High Tech High is one of the most successful schools in the world, because it's one of the best examples of a Global Learning Commons I've seen.

For Larry Rosenstock, the creation of an open, shared space intellectually has to be mirrored in the physical spaces where learning happens:

"You don't want to warehouse kids away from the world they're preparing to enter as young adults – so we have lots of kids doing internships and community service. You want the walls to be as permeable as possible."

The openness of the building design allows for the integration that drives High Tech High's intellectual mission:

178

"We're integrating several things: we're integrating students across social class (there is no streaming at High Tech High and students are selected by a blind post-code lottery); we're integrating head and hand (there are no vocational streams: technical skills are valued equally alongside academic learning): we're integrating school and community."

A key strategy for Larry and his lifelong friend and colleague Rob Riordan (High Tech High's 'Emperor of Rigor'), was to develop a design process which was more concerned with what they wouldn't allow, as what they would, in order to create a grown-up, responsible, learning culture. Consequently, no bells signal the ends of lessons; no staff-student-segregated bathrooms and no need to ask if you need to use it:

"What tends to happen in schools is that rules get added, but they don't get taken away. So, there's less and less oxygen. And a lot of the rules are really not necessary. The more rules you have, the more rules you can get around. We only have really have one rule here: do unto others as you'd have them do to you."

And there you have it. The stripped-back simplicity of a place like High Tech High has become almost counter-intuitive, so expectant are we of organisational complexity. We're frequently told that schools, like many businesses, are complex places. But it's only because we've allowed them to be. We created the silos, we created the faculties, we created the organisational manual. Over time, we just accept that it's the way things get done.

As High Tech High prove, the more complex the organisational conditions, the more basic the thought processes within them. Conversely, the simpler the structure, the more room there is for sophisticated, cross-disciplinary thinking. The beauty of having such simple structures is that the relationship between learners and teachers deepens. Most projects are team taught, so two teachers, working exclusively with 50 students over weeks, rather than hours, leads to work of the highest quality. It also means that students feel 'known', and no-one slips through the cracks. And when the project reaches its conclusion there is always a public 'exhibition of learning'.

These are extraordinary events where hundreds of parents and community members interrogate students, who have to literally 'stand by' their work, explaining concepts and recounting challenges. Students at High Tech High will tell you that there is nothing that incentivises them more than seeing better work, better appreciated than their own – they don't just tolerate feedback, they demand it.

Of course, lots of schools would claim that their students are deeply engaged in meaningful work, that parents, employers and community members play a key role in supporting students. But hardly any achieve High Tech High's level of success (Bill Gates has described it as his favourite school), mainly because they can't, or won't, make the space for collaborative planning time:

"That's one way in which we're not going to allow them to slip back into being autonomous high school teachers. Here, we see teaching as a team sport. If you want to do great work, teachers need to meet. When we built High Tech High we said 'we're going to have teachers meet with each other every day of every year, in different teams'. So, on Friday, everyone in the whole school meets, on Wednesday they look at student work... we have different configurations of common planning time which allows people to feel like, and behave like they're treated professionally."

Larry Rosenstock is in no doubt that it's easier to start a new school than to transform an existing one. Even allowing for that, what has been achieved in this series of schools close to the Mexican border is remarkable. By defying convention (Larry's favourite catchphrase is 'planning is for pessimists') and keeping their vision simple, yet steadfast, High Tech High schools are living proof that engaging students *first* pays dividends in terms of outcomes.

*****

SCA 2.0, SCIL, and High Tech High have all created vibrant, innovative and outstandingly successful learning environments. Is it purely coincidental that they have done so by putting the four values/actions that drive 'open' (share, open, free, trust) at their core?

Here are their common success strategies:

By insisting that their teachers and mentors share their learning, all three have de-privatised teaching and learning.

By opening up the commons, and by designing workspaces without walls, they have brought Edison's 'machine-shop culture' into education.

By bringing into the commons, experts, parents and investors, they have given an authenticity to the work of their students that is impossible to simulate in an enclosed classroom.

By modelling collaborative working to their students they have fostered the peer learning which is at the heart of 'open'.

By emphasising adult and real-world connections, they ensure that students are preparing for the world beyond school by being in that world.

By making their expertise and intellectual property freely available, they have created high demand from their peers and ensured that knowledge travels fast.

By seeing technology not simply as an aide to learning but as the imperative for change, they ensure that their programmes are relevant to societal needs and societal shifts.

By trusting in their staff and students, and by giving them freedom and responsibility in equal measure, they have fostered a culture of learning that rewards respectful challenge, shuns unnecessary deference, and therefore constantly stays in motion.

There is a further characteristic which unites these schools: they are determined that the 'open revolution' should not stop at the school gate. They embody the six 'Do-Its' and are determined that they should work with these engagement triggers and incorporate them into their learning designs. Most schools, sadly, have sought to exclude them.

Above all, these three case studies in creating a Global Learning Commons are inspiring examples of what happens when leaders of vision and passion are given the opportunity to defy convention. Their achievements, however, are all the more remarkable when one considers that they have been swimming against the tide of national policies in the UK, US and Australia.

All three countries, to a greater or lesser extent, have seen the route to educational transformation through varying combinations of high-stakes testing, bringing market forces into education, narrowing the range of what should be taught, and introducing payment by results. I regularly work in all three countries and to see, and hear, the effect such policies have on the morale of the teaching profession is distressing.

When most schools feel compelled to comply with top-down pressures, SCA 2.0, SCIL and High Tech High all demonstrate leadership qualities that are not deflected by such pressures, because they are driven by higher pursuits.

Driven By Moral Purpose
Our three case study leaders have a clear, distributed purpose and it is unashamedly a moral one. They believe in education as a force for social equality – Marc Lewis sees his school as a catalyst for diversity and equality in the communications industry (a notoriously white, male, middle-class occupation). They believe in values-driven learning – Larry Rosenstock is fond of quoting Thomas Jefferson's famous quote: "The purpose of public education isn't to serve the public; the purpose of public education is to create a public." And they see it as their duty to ensure that the ideas behind their successes don't remain in the petri dish, but spread virally throughout the system – witness Anne Knock's sense of responsibility to educators across Australia. They all see themselves as part of a social movement to redefine education, not simply to lead it in their own schools.

They would also, I suspect, feel comfortable being described as mavericks, but it's only because education has such a deep-seated resistance to change, that what to them seems logical appears radical to others.

The scale of innovation that we see in these three case studies represents the exception, rather than the rule. The vast majority of schools innovate incrementally. To a certain extent, this is not their fault. It takes a brave school leader to resist the pressure of government to conform. Governments generally don't do radical – at least not when it comes to how kids learn. Innovation, therefore, needs to come from schools themselves, and unless innovative new approaches become more disruptive, the reality is that they will fall further behind the pace of change of 'open'.

*****

My own experience in attempting to innovate in education came through directing two experiments in learning. The Musical Futures Programme grew out of an attempt to engage more kids in music learning. My involvement, if I'm honest, came from the personal dissatisfaction I had with the way music was taught when I attended high school, exacerbated 30 years later when my two sons had similar experiences. Funded by a UK national charity (the Paul Hamlyn Foundation), we drew on how young people learned to make music informally – in garage bands – and, thinking 'outside-in', brought those techniques into the classroom.

The heart of what we were trying to do lay in the principles laid out elsewhere in this book: making music a social and practical activity; encouraging independent and inter-dependent learning; sharing student work publicly through a specially created website. We began experimenting in about 40 schools in England, and were met initially with hostility and suspicion. How could young people play instruments without learning theory and technique? How could they improve without an expert to teach them? How would they ever learn what 'good' music was, if we 'pandered' to their tastes in hip-hop or rock music?

Gradually, through teachers seeing the transformative effect Musical Futures was having on the engagement of their students, and then spreading the word to other teachers, more schools began to adopt the approach. In 2013, 10 years after we started, we reached tipping-point: over 50 percent of all school music faculties in England had adopted Musical Futures in their teaching, and there are sister programmes in seven other countries.[3]

It's a remarkable example of how radical innovation needs to be caught, rather than imposed from above. As more school leaders saw Musical Futures in action, more of them asked 'why shouldn't this work across the whole school, in all subjects?' So Learning Futures was born, and I was again asked to lead its development.

Learning Futures followed the same principles as Musical Futures, but with a greater ambition: to see enhancing student engagement as the driver for whole school transformation. This was the point at which I realised it was one thing to change a music faculty, but quite another to change a school.

Though the conceptual base behind Learning Futures was sound, and its impact on student learning well evidenced, its spread has been hampered by one simple reality: at an organisational level, you can't change how people learn, without also changing the culture that supports innovation. The conceptual model behind Learning Futures had four essential elements:

1. Project-based Learning as the prime – but not sole – method of learning, so as to maximise student engagement.

2. Extend Learning Relationships – learning is intensely relational, so we should widen the range of mentors and experts with whom the learner has contact.

---

[3] Musical Futures is an open source initiative, so all its resources are free for any teacher to use. (www.musicalfutures.org)

3. School as Basecamp – learning becomes authentic when it is for a purpose, has impact beyond the school and supports students' communities.

4. School as Learning Commons – as seen in Chapter Four (and below).

Most of the school leaders we worked with could cope with the first three of those elements, but felt unable, unwilling, or unlicensed to commit to the fourth. That said, an increasing number of start-up schools in the UK are working with the Innovation Unit to turn their schools into learning commons, because they can see that, if schools want to see engaged students, they need to be attending an engaging school.

An 'engaging school' is one that sees the school as an integral part of its community; that welcomes mentors, experts and families into its learning spaces; is radically transparent and freely shares its expertise with others; and stimulates conversation about learning – which isn't framed within a language of targets and numbers – with the widest possible audience.

Creating a learning commons culture isn't easy, but those that have succeeded have a surprisingly consistent set of 'non-negotiables' that help to define that culture:

A culture of collaborative enquiry – educators see themselves as researchers and developers. They are encouraged to look outside education for inspiration and innovation. They are required to share those enquiries, involving students, parents, and other staff. Their learning spaces welcome the disruption of visitors, because, as Stephen Harris says 'the more students have to articulate their learning, the more they live it.' They are expected to experiment and don't face censure if their experiments don't always work. Above all else, they are given adequate time to do this.

A culture of co-construction – educators design their learning activities *with* learners, not just *for* them.

A culture of democracy – rules are kept to a minimum. Students and their parents have a right to be engaged in making decisions.

A culture of enterprise – students engage in work that matters. Schools see themselves as social enterprise hubs, creating value for their students, and their communities.

A culture of service – their role is seen, not merely to successfully move students on to the next stage of learning (important though that is), but to serve their needs as they develop as individuals, and to help them discover their responsibilities as global citizens. Equally, learning is seen as purposeful and ethical. Educators become Heng Swee Keat's 'community builders'.

'Above all, try something'

This has been a deliberately broad sweep of the challenges facing education, and educators, today. The global context described in Chapter One should demand the attention of school leaders and policy-makers everywhere. Yet the public debate on the skills teachers will need to foster in students, so that western developed nations remain economically competitive, is all but absent.

I don't want to give the impression that political leaders don't understand the importance of innovation. But you can't build innovative minds through increasing standardisation, and high stakes tests that measure little more than students' power of recall. Establishing a yardstick that can tell us how literate and numerate our young people are, compared with other nations, gives us important data that we'd be foolish to ignore. However,

187

gauging the strengths of an education system by PISA and TIMSS comparisons alone is like assessing the health of a patient by only taking their temperature.

The US academic Yong Zhao brings a unique perspective to the education and economic competitiveness connection. He was schooled in China, but is now one of the foremost writers on global education systems, working out of America. At the end of 2012 he published a provocative but compelling blog post: 'Numbers Can Lie: What TIMSS and PISA Truly Tell Us, if Anything?'

His hard-to-refute argument is that American students have performed badly at international tests of academic ability, for more than 50 years. Yet during that time they have led the world in creativity and enterprise: fifth in global competitiveness; second (behind Sweden) in the global creativity index; first in the number of patents filed. The current giants of US innovation were schooled at a time when American education was proud of its liberal arts tradition. The clear and present danger must be that, 10 years from now, the products of the current, more conservative, exam-focused system will be ill-equipped to maintain the reputation of the most innovative nation on earth.

Even those who lead schools with high rankings are aware of the long-term dangers of being driven by numbers. Paul Fisher, Head of Oakridge Primary School in Stafford, England, saw his standardised test scores among the best in the country in 2012. Dismissing the showering of praise, Paul instead argued for the removal of formal testing, claiming that their students' successes owed more to the 90 field trips they'd undertaken rather than relentless test preparation. "It is a shame in this country that we've got a Government that's trying to take us back to the Edwardian period with a focus on feeding children facts. Do we want a society that's great at pub quizzes or one that's great at thinking and problem solving?"

I've argued throughout this book that we need to radically rethink how we manage learning, in education and the world of work, in response to 'open'. The changes that have transformed the way we learn informally are also the ones that have shifted the balance of economic power globally. In many countries we appear to be responding to the challenges of the knowledge economy, by reinforcing the industrialisation of education. This tactic might have worked well when we needed factory hands, but it is failing us now.

Giving the commencement address at Oglethorpe University in 1932 (a period of great economic uncertainty) Franklin D. Roosevelt, remarked:

"The country needs and, unless I mistake its temper, the country demands bold, persistent experimentation. It is common sense to take a method and try it: If it fails, admit it frankly and try another. But above all, try something."

You may not agree with my arguments here, but there is surely little doubt that we need to try something new. Because what we've been doing in recent years in most developed countries is to reheat 19th and 20th-century thinking and serve it up as a forward-looking approach. The world, however, no longer conforms to 19th and 20th-century models of development. Why then, do we think that we'll find the answers by looking backwards?

As the great educational philosopher, John Dewey, once said, "If we teach today's students as we taught yesterday's, we rob them of tomorrow."

Chapter Nine

Open and You

Before examining what 'open' might mean for the way you, your employees, or your children learn in the future, let's return briefly to the themes introduced at the start of this book.

The belt-tightening following the global financial crisis has disproportionately affected the poor and the young. Despite the best efforts of successive UK governments, for example, the number of Britons in relative poverty has consistently risen since 1980. In 1970, CEOs in America earned 39 times the average salary of their company's employees. By 2000, that multiplier had risen to 1,039 times the average worker's salary. By 2011, the one percent of wealthiest Americans, who so angered the Occupy movement, controlled 40 percent of the nation's wealth.

Globally, young people (aged 15-24) constitute a quarter of the world's working-age population, yet they make up almost half of all those unemployed. Here's a depressing stat: one in five of the entire world's young live on less than $1 a day. On top of the economic disadvantages they face, they are perhaps the first generation for whom the phrase 'natural' resources has a hollow ring to it – the solutions to the multiple energy and environmental crises will simply *have* to be found within the next 20 to 30 years, or our current college kids face an old age not worth imagining.

There's No New Normal

We therefore face a host of global challenges, and relying upon what we already know has limited value. The thing we need most in the midst of an 'open revolution' is an open mind.

I'm personally thankful, therefore, that so many young people, despite the hand they've been dealt, are so lacking in cynicism, and so selfless in their determination to find new answers to the age-old question: how shall we live? If the 1980s spawned the 'me' generation, driven by material need, they are being followed by the 'we' generation, driven by a set of values and ethics that put us to shame. All we really have to do is not get in their way.

Creative solutions to the many challenges ahead will require divergent, creative and cross-disciplinary learning. Fortunately, the kinds of social learning now emerging encourage us to think differently. Divergence in thinking demands a diversity of thinkers. A borderless learning commons, therefore, becomes critical to solving trans-national problems. A commons welcomes newcomers, an enclosure keeps them out.

Frustrated by a lack of impetus and new ideas from our historic institutions, some in the Global Learning Commons are thinking big. The author Don Tapscott, for example, envisages a 'global solutions network' – a multi-stakeholder global collection of activist groups (some of whom I've highlighted in these pages), as a better, more agile model to solve the global crises facing us than the post-war founded global 'representative' organisations:

"Now we can move towards a different model that embraces representative democracy, but it's based on multiple stakeholders, and it's characterised by a culture of public deliberation and of active citizenship. What an exciting time! ... (Change) is not going to come about

191

solely by our great leaders selling a new vision of how we can cooperate... down to their populations... It's going to come about through millions and millions of people participating and bringing about real change." [1]

During the 2013 general election, Italian politics was stunned by the sudden emergence of the 'Movimento 5 Stelle' (5-Star Movement). Formed in 2009, and led by comedian Beppe Grillo, the party has no offices – it exists entirely on the internet – and members chose their candidates through online primaries. It advocates 'direct democracy' where people vote for each initiative, not leaving such decisions to their elected representatives. In the 2013 general election 'Movimento 5 Stelle' became the largest party in Italy's parliament, winning 25 percent of the vote. It is an astonishing story, and one which we are likely to see repeated as Europe continues to simmer.

There is an urgency, and uncertainty, surrounding the future of these new forms of networked movements, and concerns that they can accelerate the growth of extremist political parties, from the left and right. Corporations have vested interests, political parties expect to lead, so we can anticipate resistance. One of the features of distributed networks, however, is that they are constantly in flux. Occupy's activism hasn't gone away, it's just become more horizontal. Instead of high-profile city-centre gatherings, there are now tens of thousands of low-profile actions bringing citizens together, here to prevent a house foreclosure, there to rebuild after Hurricane Sandy, all the while helping to fashion new forms of democracy.

These networks are not content with lying dormant between four to five-year election cycles, nor are they content to only care about domestic national issues. Groups like Avaaz.org, and

---

[1] Don Tapscott, speaking at the RSA 28th February 2013

even Anonymous, realise that their strength and security lie in their numbers and global reach.

How then, can learning adapt to such seismic changes? How can businesses and places of formal learning remain relevant, amid a torrent of informal, do-it-yourself initiatives? How can we foster the principles of collaboration, creativity and innovation needed to meet the challenges we face? Before I offer some practical suggestions for those working in businesses, education, or 'just' bringing up kids, let me share a couple of over-arching, inevitable, directional shifts that we all have to work with, not against. Be warned, for it's about to get ugly.

From Pedagogy to Heutagogy

There must be some unwritten academic maxim somewhere that if you want to dissuade people from attempting to understand how learning works, you give them the worst names you can think of. I will attempt to explain this in simple language, but let's start with a technical announcement:

Though it was happening anyway, 'open' has accelerated the shift from pedagogy, to andragogy, to heutagogy.

There, aren't you glad I told you that? Notwithstanding the fact that I managed to combine the three ugliest words in the English language in a single sentence, I like to think there's quite a profound thought in there. The word pedagogy derives from Greek and, literally translated, means 'to lead the child'; andragogy is translated as 'to lead the man (adult)'; heutagogy means 'to lead to find'. I know, that's not much clearer. But, if we look at commonly-used interpretations, it gets better.

In pedagogy, the learner is led to a conclusion determined by the teacher, informed by the teacher's knowledge and beliefs – it could be termed 'instructional learning'. In andragogy, though the destination may be decided by the tutor, the route involves greater learner involvement, acknowledging the

193

importance of relevance, motivation and problem-solving. Although andragogy is a term open to many interpretations, let's use it here to denote 'self-directed learning. In heutagogy, there is not necessarily a defined destination, nor a prescribed route – it is 'self-determined learning'.

These shifts in how we're learning mirror the bigger shifts in how we're living. We are moving from being compliant citizens, being told what is good for us, to informed actors who are determining our own futures. As society inevitably becomes more open, the way we learn in the future simply has to reflect those shifts. Changes in learning are both a reflection, and a consequence, of how we now want to live.

The shift, from instruction to self-determination, is also happening because that's the path we've been taking when we learn informally. When we're learning for fun, we surf not knowing where it will take us, just doing it for the joy of discovery. If we find something of interest to us, we share it with others, in 'communities of discovery'. If enough people pool their findings they might even collectively come up with 'new' knowledge, or insights.

Whilst this 'higher-order' learning requires discipline and greater learner responsibility, it would be wrong to see it as only for grown-ups. I have seen children in the primary stages of their education quite happily take the path of self-determination. Ewan McIntosh, educator and social learning expert, argues that young students should be not just 'problem solvers' but 'problem finders'. In 2011, Ewan worked with 10,000 students from 98 schools who were all invited to find a problem, and then prototype solutions (everything from water filters for polluted rivers to clothing made out of potato chip packets). So, heutagogy is equally applicable to children as it is to adults. It's defined by approach, not age.

From Factoids to Deep Knowledge

The second shift in direction is that knowing is no longer reliant upon our recollection of information, and more about our ability to create and connect new ideas. Traditional, instructional pedagogy involves the transference of knowledge or facts from expert to novice. For centuries we had no alternative but to have that transference take place in a classroom. But now that we can instantaneously get facts from a Google search, do we need to place such dependence upon our powers of recall? Could this lead to liberation of the teacher's role, in helping us connect data, guiding us to make sense of facts, and create new ideas? Apparently not.

In January 2011, the new English Secretary of State for Education advocated a return to the teaching of facts to students. If you ever needed a reason to keep politics out of learning, here it was. I decided to blog about this, under the pretence that I'd had a sneak preview of a new Google app called 'Factoid'. I described how, by combining the search tool powering Google's powerful Adsense technology – which links email text to suggested ads – with their plans to digitise the world's books, it would no longer be necessary to remember facts.

I had invented a series of filters: Significant Dates (history); Connecting Countries (geography); Add It Up (statistics); Quotable Quotes (literature), which would offer up facts to feed into your essay, say, on the French Revolution. In the future, I concluded, we wouldn't have to find facts, they'd find us. The more I made it up, the more excited I got about this eminently feasible piece of kit. At the time of writing, Google haven't yet unveiled such a tool (though if they subsequently do, please treat this description, Sergey, as my stake in the IP, and you'll find me sipping cocktails on Richard Branson's tropical island). [2]

---

[2] I posted assuming that the Google Books settlement on fair use with the Authors Guild would signal the go-ahead in Google's strategy. At the time of

It seems ridiculous that an education minister should call for a return to 19th-century, fact-based learning methods, while employers are looking for people who can critically analyse, ask important questions, and make connections between facts, rather than regurgitate them. Politicians do seem to spend inordinate amounts of time making ineffectual policy changes to how we might be taught, and then defending such policies, rather than reflecting the transformation in how we're actually learning, and then freeing us up to do so. As James Surowiecki noted in 'The Wisdom of Crowds':

> "It's easier for individuals to create explanations to justify the way things are than to imagine how they might be different."

So, as this book draws to a close, allow me to summarise, and suggest how, by going 'open', we might imagine things to be different.

The Bit That Would Have Saved You From Having To Read the Whole Book

Almost everything that determines our future – societal governance, the economy, industry, the environment, our education system, and much more – is being fundamentally re-examined. All of those pillars are likely to look very different in 20, if not 10, years from now.

The institutions, which represent those pillars, are under scrutiny because we are discovering new ways to connect, and new reasons for doing so. The connections become possible through the opening up of knowledge. The democratisation of

---

writing, the issue of copyright infringement is still being fought over by lawyers. Notwithstanding legal battles, with the coming of the European and Digital Public Library of America projects, my point, I believe, is still pertinent.

learning is driving disintermediation: we no longer need the doctor to tell us what is wrong with us, or the salesperson to tell us which product to buy, or the educator to tell us the answer. We can help each other come to those conclusions.

Disintermediation means that pop stars can have direct conversations with their fans, and would-be pop stars can sell their products directly to their would-be fans, without the need for a record company. More significantly, perhaps, disintermediation allows corporations to have a direct conversation with customers, without the need for market research, and governments to centralise control without the need for non-governmental agencies, or quangos.

Most importantly we, as employees, consumers, learners and concerned citizens, are discovering that we can talk to each other, and learn from each other without the need for those intermediaries. This is heady stuff, and it's hard to imagine a scenario where we'd willingly hand this new-found power back.

Along with the good stuff, however, disintermediation also means fewer jobs for people who used to work in those intermediary roles. A business that once would have needed to hire a local IT company to build its website, can now directly engage freelancers from any part of the world. Authors that once needed agents and publishers to find their audience can now do it themselves. Disintermediation is having a seismic effect on employment, and, therefore economies, throughout the world. And no one knows how it will work itself out. Only those intermediaries that can add value will survive.

In itself, all this would represent a paradigm shift – an irreversible economic, political and societal off-axis tilt. It is in the reasons for connecting, however, that the real revolution resides. Because disintermediation allows us to take independent and collaborative actions, which enable us to better control our lives, and become more autonomous, and therefore more engaged, in how we work, live and learn. We have rediscovered mutual trust, become intoxicated by the power of reciprocal generosity, and felt liberated by our lessening reliance upon institutions, and by the power of sharing.

Exemplified by a myriad of civic movements, self-help groups and social enterprises, and powered through 'open' principles, we have rediscovered the spirit of the commons. It turns out that participating and learning in the commons is borderless, immediate, purposeful, informal, playful, transparent, and authentic. In fact, we like it so much that we wonder why the companies we work for, the schools we attend, and the public and private sector institutions we deal with, seem so restrictive by comparison.

The early adopters – our most innovative companies, schools, colleges and institutions – are already incorporating the values and motivations found in *Open*. They understand the need to radically change how they operate. The best schools and colleges similarly see their futures in opening up learning to a much wider range of participants. They're restructuring the teacher/learner relationship to allow for more autonomy and collegiality, more independence and interdependence in learning.

These organisations are in the vanguard of coming to terms with the new reality, the end of command-and-control. Others seem to be either unaware of the need to change, or are hoping it will somehow blow over. I suspect the largest group is the remainder: organisations, centres of learning and mildly bewildered parents who instinctively grasp the magnitude of change but don't know how best to navigate their way through it.

So, allow me to conclude with some practical advice for those who want to become 'open', but need some help doing it.

Open Learning in Business

1. Engage in Engagement

Companies that don't place a high priority on engagement will never create engaging places to work in. We've already seen how vital employee engagement is to productivity, innovation and worker retention. You won't know how engaged your employees are unless you ask them, so if you don't do so already, regularly measure engagement.

Engagement starts with a conversation. The conversations can't just be internal – though that also has to happen. Employees will engage if the company itself engages – with its customers/clients and its geographic and online community. Becoming a social business has a transformative effect on engagement. Don't see engagement as a luxury to be invested in only when the sun is shining – engagement is vital to innovation and to the creation of new products and services.

2. Value Values

Similarly, companies that are only interested in creating shareholder value end up eating themselves. Companies that are committed to changing the world for the better will flourish. Simply complying with legal requirements for social responsibility isn't enough. Open learning and citizen journalism means there is now nowhere to hide unethical practices. If the hacktivists don't get you, then your customers will. As the head of business development at Proctor & Gamble said, "People are going to want, and be able, to find out about the citizenship of a brand, whether it is doing the right things socially, economically and environmentally."

Ethics and corporate social responsibility will increasingly impact upon employee engagement, because employees are also consumers and seek the same thing. The smart companies now support staff volunteering – in work time – in the local community, because of its impact on employee engagement. Building a culture of service is a lot more fun than maintaining a culture of servitude.

If, however, employee engagement is not a big enough reason to broaden your value priorities, consider this: there is growing evidence that demonstrating a strong social responsibility is correlated to improved financial performance, and there is a clear link between being listed in the FTSE4Good or Dow Jones Sustainability Indexes and share performance. It wasn't, I suspect, pure altruism that drove Steve Jobs to say, "The creative economy is the future of the world. Let's make a better one together".

3. Trust in Trust

In researching this book it seems that straddling the knowing-doing gap of trust is one of the stiffest challenges facing business leaders. They know they should do it, but too often they just can't bring themselves to do it. It's partly because trust tends towards absolutism: having partial trust in someone, is the same as having none. This is not to say that trust should be naively applied – trust and responsibility need to go hand-in-hand. But in an age of openness, a company that does not trust its workforce is unlikely to gain the trust of its customers.

Trust is often the first casualty in an economic depression, and the public loss of trust in major corporations since 2008 will take years to restore. Warren Buffet believes 'it takes 20 years to build a reputation, and five minutes to ruin it', but making your company a social business is seen as an attractive option for those seeking to build their reputations quickly. You can't claim to be a social business, however, if you don't demonstrate trust in each and every employee.

That means you'll just have to trust that they're learning socially, and using social media tools in the best interests of your business. If they're discovering what your customers really think of your business, that's time well spent. If they're learning how to do their job better, don't freak out because they appear to be using Twitter. In fact, get a Twitter account yourself – you'll soon see how useful it is to your own learning. Of course, some may abuse that trust, but the majority will feel connected, valued and engaged. Those sorts of people tend not to watch the clock. Besides, if you create a results-only work environment does it really matter that they ordered a Groupon voucher on work time?

4. Learn About Learning

While pretty much every CEO knows how budgeting works, how many of them know how learning works? Yet knowing how to build the curiosity, imagination, creativity, knowledge and skills of your workforce is arguably more important than the ability to understand complex financial data. The speed at which companies are required to innovate raises the learning stakes. CEOs can't simply delegate the responsibility for learning to others. They have to know how to provide learning opportunities, and they have to be learners themselves. An enlightened and highly visible commitment to organisational learning not only built the Edison empire, but also inspired employee loyalty and engagement.

So the lesson is, promote learning, not work. If workers – like those who worked for Edison – feel like they're learning, they don't feel like they're working. They'll more often be in 'flow', rather than the 'pretend-attend' state they perfected in their high-school careers. And, as we've seen repeatedly throughout this book, the implications of learning in the social space insist that learners are given more autonomy – give learners the right to roam.

An innovative learning environment needs a diverse community of learners. Creative breakthroughs come from challenging questions, not conformity. So an open learning organisation creates a culture of respectful challenge, has a high tolerance of mavericks, and avoids mimics.

Collaboration is the bedrock of learning. The Global Learning Commons is inclusive. The most effective learning is found in projects seeking to solve intractable problems. Proctor and Gamble's Connect and Develop is a graphic illustration of the power of learning through crowdsourcing. So, always seek to co-construct solutions, with whoever wants to play.

Learning isn't just for company elites. It was Telus and Xerox engineers whose sharing via social learning platforms saved their companies fortunes, not middle managers. 3M gave all of its employees 15 percent free time, not just the top scientists. Allowing everyone the freedom to follow their interests sends an important message: that good ideas can be found everywhere, by anyone.

Welcome failure – simply having different sets of eyeballs wasn't enough to make 3M's post-it notes happen. It also needed a freedom to fail culture. We can only be creative when we're not afraid to make mistakes. Those failure rates at Google and 3M (36 percent and 50 percent respectively) are what make them two of the most innovative companies in the world. Try re-labelling mistakes as 'learning moments', like they do at WD-40, and take away the fear of failure. And make sure everybody knows about it when you have learning moments too.

5. Open Up Your Business

Open organisations – Edison believed in machine shops, not silos. The smart companies, like Valve are opting for fluid org charts - forming teams to work on self-chosen projects, and then disbanding. Facebook established 'Hackamonth', so that engineers who had been on the same project for over a year could work for a month on any other project that needed help. The result has been new energies, new perspectives. If you want innovation to flourish, you need learning to stay fresh, not departmental groupthink.

Open culture – radical transparency is fast becoming the default position for innovative, socially responsible companies. Remember Tony Hsieh of Zappos.com?   He advocates the 'happiness principle': 'You can't have happy customers, unless you have happy staff'. And urging his staff to 'be real' is the key to good staff-customer relationships. You can't be real, unless you have a culture of transparency. Being transparent means letting go of command and control. That carries risks. But the alternative – creating communications enclosures and plugging the gaps where unhappiness leaks out – is just exhausting.

Open data – the irresistible demand is to make data free. A company like OpenCorporates.com – 'the open database of the corporate world' – has publicly-accessible data on 51 million companies throughout the world. Pressure groups relentlessly badger our governments to release information. Businesses will eventually have to open up, so why not get ahead of the curve?
As Patrick McKenna argued earlier, it's impossible to prevent intellectual property from being leaked, hacked, or pirated. However, that's not the point: the capital value lies, not in the information, but in how you use it. Increasingly, businesses will release data in order to understand its value from the way it's being used. The old advice – to never give away anything you can sell – has been turned on its head by the open source

movement. Going 'open' has transformed the fortunes of most of the companies featured earlier – it could do the same for you.

Open Learning in Education

There's much of the above that also applies to formal education. My advice to school leaders who are serious about engaging their students is this: you won't have to worry about their engagement if you get yours right. Make school an engaging place to learn, not the exam factories we so frequently observe these days. Your learners will be passionate about collaborating, making and doing things, just like they do in the world outside school/college; though it seems obvious that the surest way to prepare students for life beyond formal education is to make education as much like that life as possible. It takes a brave education leader, however, to defy the current obsession with testing.

The great educator, John Holt, once likened over-testing to a gardener pulling up a plant by its roots so that he could see how well it was growing. If a love of learning were a human right (and I contend that it should be) our courts would be overflowing with abuse of rights claims from our young.

This is where educators face their own knowing-doing gap. Instinctively, they know that if the goal is the engagement of every single student, the exam results should take care of themselves. How could we not become knowledgeable about things we are passionate about, and absorbed in? But the safest course of action is to aim for 'coverage' of the curriculum, and the filling of endless worksheets, which do little other than document students' increasing disenchantment with learning.

Values also tend to be overlooked in formal education. By this I don't mean the study of ethics, but rather the often-missed opportunity of values-led learning. In the US, there is greater commitment to 'service learning' (connecting the curriculum to local and global needs through purposeful projects) than in most countries.

When done well, service learning increases the engagement of students, and increases their sense of agency. It was a lack of agency that drove many of the English rioters of 2011 to ransack their high streets. I like to think that more service learning in English schools may have made more of them think twice before setting their cities alight. See your school as the base camp for learning, and get them learning out there, where they live. More than anything, schools should value the outside-in perspective that creating a learning commons brings.

The expertise that lies just beyond their gates is too valuable to ignore. Businesses, community groups and parents – especially parents – carry skills and life experiences that can help young adults make sense of the world they're joining. Over 2,000 potential mentors and experts exist in every high-school parent body, most of whom would be happy to volunteer their time and effort to help their school, yet how often do we use them?

All of the above builds what Larry Rosenstock calls 'adult-world connections'. If more of our schools (and colleges) were committed to this single goal, we wouldn't see the shockingly low engagement rates outlined in Chapter Five. Instead, partly because we have allowed ourselves to be terrified about the safety of our young people in schools, we make our schools as forbidding as possible.

If you're an educational leader reading this, I hope I've encouraged you to bring the Global Learning Commons we see in the social space into your place of learning. But for even the best intentioned of leaders, knowing where to start can be daunting. Here's my advice: simply resolve to remove every physical, organisational and cultural manifestation of a learning enclosure you can find, and open it up to the commons philosophy. Here's what I mean:

Physical – don't allow any educator to organise rows of desks - nothing reminds students of their relative anonymity, and their place in the hierarchy, than serried ranks. Don't allow any teacher to have a closed-door policy – make learning a public activity. Where possible, eliminate dividing walls between classes to build a collaborative culture – instead, think machine-shop and studios, with discrete spaces for experimenting, presenting, researching, and, yes, relaxing.

Don't think that high fences, security cameras, intercoms and metal detectors guarantee safety – as the massacre at Sandy Hook Elementary School sadly demonstrates, schools are powerless in the face of a determined, deranged individual. The side effects, however, of such measures are to reinforce the impression that students already have: of school being set apart from the real world.

Organisational – perhaps the biggest enclosure of all is the schedule (timetable) that governs learning. Moving kids around each time a bell rings every 50 minutes, only reminds them that they are cogs in an industrial machine, and destroys any attempt to deepen learning, so get rid of the atomised schedule. While you're at it, get rid of the bell too. And the tannoy announcements. This is a learning commons, not a prison. Commit to giving students the freedom and responsibilities of adults, and they'll behave like them.

Cultural – because of the workloads and isolation forced upon most teachers, schools have a hard time with collaboration. But it doesn't have to be like that. Schools are generally free to organise themselves as they see fit. So strive for collegiality. Don't allow teachers to simply 'deliver' learning. They need to be designers and researchers of learning. And when they're designing, please remember the six 'imperatives of social learning' listed in Chapter Six: Do it yourself; Do it now; Do it with friends; Do unto others; Do it for fun; Do it for the world to see. These are the drivers of their own learning when they're not in school or college. If you want to build a learning commons, make use of them.

Make time for collaborative planning. Don't allow staff to design learning at the end of the day – that's when they're tired, cranky and wondering why they got into teaching. Instead, start the day when they're fresh and feeling good about themselves, with professional development.

The great schools and colleges that I've seen all have an obsessional desire to understand what great learning looks like. They talk about learning, among teachers and with students, all the time. They constantly innovate and they're not afraid of getting it wrong. No student ever had his entire education ruined because of a learning innovation that didn't come off. But I can show you plenty of students whose curiosity and imagination were strangled by being trapped in a repetitive, uninspiring, unimaginative learning enclosure.

All this may seem like I'm asking teachers to work a lot harder. In fact, most of the above suggestions are about stripping things back. For example, too often teachers feel they have to 'perform' in class. They spend countless hours preparing, fretting about how to make their lessons more engaging. In reality, most of the time they're doing all the work, and their kids are hardly doing any.

When I led the Musical Futures project mentioned in the previous chapter, one of our biggest challenges lay in convincing teachers that learning would still take place if they weren't directing things from the front of the class. Getting them to stand back and allow students to learn from each other went against all of their training. At the same time, I'd heard about Sugata Mitra's 'Hole In The Wall' experiment in New Delhi, which was seeing remarkable progress being made by children from slums in learning to use computers, without any adult input. I went to meet with Professor Mitra, and it was clear that both our initiatives were improving students' learning simply by getting out of their way. The wide-scale adoption of our respective approaches across differing cultural contexts would suggest that the capacity of students to teach themselves, aided by appropriate technologies, has been under appreciated and under reported. Does this mean teachers will soon become redundant? Absolutely not. It just means that they will have to accommodate the social desire to shift from pedagogy to heutagogy, and support learners to become more independent, and self-determined.

Open Futures

There's still one constituent in all of this that we haven't really addressed: you.

Yes, I really do mean you, so stop looking around. Because how you – as a parent, a worker, a human being and, above all, as a learner – respond to the challenges outlined here will largely determine if 'open' is an Arab Spring or a Bay of Pigs, an iPad or a Sinclair C5.

In other words, this is a unique opportunity for the concerned citizen. After decades of slumber, something stirs. We former couch potatoes have discovered that it's a lot more fun to watch some TED talks, or take part in an online campaign, than watching reruns of soaps. In fact, we're doing so much of this stuff, that some point to the dangers of 'clicktivism' – believing you're politically engaged simply by hitting the 'like'

208

button on a Facebook page. For me, whether 10 million clicks on an Avaaz.org campaign is any less 'authentic' than a protest march of a hundred or so misses the point. The important thing is to participate. Don't worry if you don't know a meetup from a mic check. And do not, under any circumstances, believe any of that digital native/digital immigrant nonsense.

The terms 'digital natives' and 'digital immigrants' were first coined by Marc Prensky. The former applies to anyone born after the invention of the iPod. The latter applies to the rest of us. Younger users are deemed to be completely fluent in speaking digital, while the rest of us speak haltingly, and with a heavy accent. While these stereotypes have become fixed in our collective consciousness and offer an easy way out when over-50s can't be bothered learning how to programme the video recorder, they have no basis in fact.

Recent research suggests that attitudes to technology are independent of age. The average age of a video gamer is 37, and rising. Sure, adolescents might be a little more dexterous in their deployment of technology, but content is still king. It's not the app that you use it's what you do on it that matters. So, jump in, and don't worry – nobody's yet managed to break the internet.

Another source of parental angst is the amount of time our kids spend online. Two of the wisest experts out there, Cathy Davidson and Sherry Turkle, recently published well-researched, yet sharply contrasting, analyses of how technology affects young people's desire and abilities to socially interact with each other.[3] This goes to the heart of the current dilemma for parents: we know how important technology is for our kids' futures, but we worry about the side effects. We therefore fret about whether they're spending too much, or too little, time online. Since

[3] Davidson, C. *Now You See It: How Technology and Brain Science Will Transform Schools and Business for the 21st Century* (2011) Penguin Books; Turkle, S. *Alone Together* (2011) Basic Books

there's no incontrovertible evidence that would guide us here, you may as well relax, they'll find the answer themselves.

Do ask them, however, to share their social learning with you – it will give you a glimpse of the future they're facing, and it's often far more interesting than the stuff they have to do at school, or college. Visit sites like Elance or oDesk. You will immediately understand the scale of the challenge: in the early part of the 20th century we competed for work against the people in our towns; in the second half of the century, the competition was initially regional, and then national; now, it's global.

If you accept my analysis of the changing employment market and the competition we're facing from rapidly developing nations, then it's hard to know what to say to advise our kids. The global auction for skills suggests that it's going to be hard for them to find jobs. So, they may as well create their own. Entrepreneurship will be at a premium, because it's entrepreneurship that enables innovation to flourish.

So, think about what this means for your child's social, and formal, learning environments. If you're choosing a school by its examination results alone, is that really going to be in your child's best interests? There's no great secret to improving a school's test scores. But is repeatedly drilling your kids to pass a test what they actually need for an entrepreneurial future? Might it not be better to find a school that will allow them to find their passion and build the communicative, collaborative, and imaginative skills that are already key to our collective futures?

Over the years, I've sat in countless discussions where we've tried to identify the agency that will bring about radical change in educational policy, by looking forwards, not backwards. Will it be the teaching profession, or business leaders? Increasingly, I believe it will be parents. Parents, because of their voting power, are probably the only people that politicians will listen too. They need to become more vocal, and reclaim the ground they have lost in the debate around what good schooling looks like. Along the way, the language we use to describe learning has been reduced to letters and numbers.

We know, from repeated market research studies, that if you stop people in the street and ask them what they look for in a perfect cup of coffee they will usually say the same thing – strong tasting, black, big aroma. When they're at home they invariably make it weak and milky. As it is with coffee, so it is with the language of learning.

Most parents, I believe, would prefer to know about their child's confidence, their sense of well-being, their capacity for independent thought, or their ability to ask critical questions – the language of milky coffee. Instead, parents only know the language of black coffee, because that's all they hear. Are they on target for good grades? Are they getting enough homework? What were their last test scores?

Prescriptive educational policies, like 'No Child Left Behind' and 'Common Core Standards' in the US, the school league tables in the UK, and the introduction of standardised tests and a national curriculum in Australia, may have given the impressions that politicians are doing something about education. But along the way they are closing down conversations with parents about how their children should learn, because of the obsession with numbers. That refocusing of language and priorities will not come about through politicians admitting the error of their ways. Parents will have to regain the initiative, and find their voices.

A Candle, Not An Apple

When Rupert Murdoch sold the social networking site, MySpace, for $35m – just six percent of what he paid for it – he reflected that 'we screwed up in every way possible'. The site's users – predominantly musicians and bands sharing their music to gain a wider audience – reacted badly to the media mogul's presence in their commons. Sensing imminent enclosure in pursuit of Murdoch's self-interest, they simply upped and left. It was an example of how strong the philosophy of a true commons can be, and how susceptible it can be to over-exploitation. A new way of looking at this tension between common good and self-interest was advanced by Lawrence Lessig, Professor of Law at Harvard Law School.

Speaking in 2004, Lessig – who was one of the architects behind the Creative Commons movement – revisited the arguments, which were used to enclose British grazing land, known as 'the tragedy of the commons'. Put simply, the tragedy occurs when livestock owners try to squeeze in an extra few cattle, or sheep, on the commons. Their personal yield goes up. But if everyone does it the land becomes over-grazed, and useless.

This argument was famously rehashed by Garrett Hardin, in 1968, in an essay which called for enforced limits on population growth. He reasoned that, since we are driven by self-interest, it is only human nature to try to take the most out of a shared utility:

> "…this is the conclusion reached by each and every rational herdsman sharing a commons. Therein is the tragedy. Each man is locked into a system that compels him to increase his herd without limit – in a world that is limited. Ruin is the destination toward which all men rush, each pursuing his own best interest in a society that believes in the freedom of the commons. Freedom in a commons brings ruin to all."[4]

---

[4] Hardin, G. *The Tragedy Of The Commons*, Science 13th December 1968: Vol. 162

Lessig, however, draws the important distinction between properties that are rivalrous and non-rivalrous. The grass on a commons is rivalrous – if my cattle eat it, yours can't, and you and your cattle suffer as a result. Similarly, if I take a bite out of your apple, that's my gain, your loss. But learning is a non-rivalrous property. If I share an idea with you, you gain, but not at my expense. I still have that knowledge. Knowledge can be likened to the light from a candle: I can light many other candles without losing the original source of light.

It's hard to overstate the power of this idea. It lies at the core of *Open*, and has often been the source of bitter dispute as attempts to control not merely the expression of ideas, but the idea itself, periodically occur. We see it most recently in the battle for 'control' of the internet. Those who would seek to create learning enclosures, by restricting our ability to share all that we know, would claim that such enclosures are 'for our own good'. Governments are trying to protect the populace from cyber-terrorists, publishers from pirates, while corporations need those restrictions to maximise shareholder return. The consequence is that where we find knowledge, and whom we learn skills from, needs to be tightly controlled. Their fear is that, now that we have the means to do so, if they allow us to learn from each other, they've lost authority and control in equal measure. Worse, only they know who the bad guys are.

This is not to say that we can afford to be naive. There are bad people out there who will attempt to do bad things unless the force of the law prevents them. But neither should we allow our collective knees to be jerked by simplistic scare stories. Paedophilia wasn't invented after the internet, would-be terrorists used to share plans by using homing pigeons, and not every under-18-year-old illegally downloads books, music and films.

The validity of Hardin's position, and whether the freedom of the commons is in fact a tragedy, really comes down to your assessment of human nature: if all that drives us is self-interest, then freedom may indeed bring ruin to us all. I've tried to show throughout this book, that we've entered into a period where our better selves can emerge. We are taking to the streets, each other's houses, and the internet forums, in large numbers, partly to show that we're driven by higher ideals; to show that the politics of fear, greed, competition and distrust no longer represent us, they merely repress us.

We have good cause to be optimistic about the social movement that has barely started. Our young people, despite the enormity of the financial and environmental mess we're leaving them, seem remarkably upbeat about their capacity to save the world. As social media has grown, so has our confidence that we can use it to help others. As informal learning moves mainstream, so we have recognised that learning by doing is just as important as learning by reading. The advent of the video tutorial does not diminish the power of the written word. There will always be a monetary value in expertise, but that value is affected by scarcity, and 'open' now means that expertise is everywhere.

It is not just the speed of technological transformation that will determine how we cope with the changes we're facing, but the values and actions that we ourselves hold dear. Those values and actions, which we're cultivating in the social space, will need to benignly infect the way we work, live, and learn. I'm convinced they can. We need, however, to be brave, and be willing to jettison the assumptions that we formed when the world turned rather more slowly than it does today.

Perhaps most remarkably, we are at a point where open learning can bring about a world envisaged with great prescience and eloquence by Thomas Jefferson when he reasoned that freely sharing our learning was not only the highest of aspirations, it was our natural state of being:

"He who receives an idea from me, receives instruction himself without lessening mine; as he who lights his taper at mine, receives light without darkening me. That ideas should freely spread from one to another over the globe, for the moral and mutual instruction of man, and improvement of his condition, seems to have been peculiarly and benevolently designed by nature, when she made them, like fire, expansible over all space, without lessening their density in any point, and like the air in which we breathe, move, and have our physical being, incapable of confinement or exclusive appropriation." [5]

'Open' is beginning to reshape our political institutions. It's starting to challenge the dominance of free-market capitalism. It offers a new way for companies and corporations to do businesses. It has shaken up higher education and will eventually do the same for our schooling system. This is already an impressive set of works-in-progress, but the potential of 'open' is even greater. It could, in time, rescue the planet from the threat of self-destruction, because the scientific advances required to ensure our survival, can only achieve scale and sustainability if we treat that knowledge as common property.

Open learning gives the rural farmer in Kenya the same opportunity for self-improvement as the middle-class kid in California. It also gives them the chance to connect and understand each other a little better. Every time we gather in the learning commons, we chip away at fear and prejudice, and we

---

[5] Thomas Jefferson, writing to Isaac MacPherson 13th August 1813

glimpse a future that's collaborative, not simply competitive. We're lighting candles, not biting apples.

On one level, *Open* is about changing national values and corporate priorities. On another level, it's deeply personal.

For this book, and this social movement, is about the story we choose to tell ourselves. That story used to be told to us by others. It said 'if you want to learn new skills, be better at your job, improve your community, you need the experts to tell you how to do it. Not everyone can get access to that expertise, but life in the information age was never meant to be fair. There can only be winners if there are losers'.

Open tells a different story. It says 'we can work this out for ourselves, level the playing field, share what we know, trust in our creativity, have fun doing it, and we'll let you know when we need your help'. Not everyone has yet heard that story, because we're only just grasping the incredible force we hold in our collective heads, hands and hearts. But, as more of us reach for the off button on that TV remote, and turn to each other to share our story, the more we begin to believe in ourselves. It's a story whose ending we cannot predict, because we're literally making it up as we go along. That's why it's so exciting, because the learning lies in the telling of the story.

Acknowledgements

This book began life as a result of a chance encounter, at Heathrow airport, in 2010, with Sir Ken Robinson. I've known Ken for a long time - we worked together to establish the Liverpool Institute for Performing Arts in the 1990s - and he was particularly supportive when, in 2000, I decided to work for myself. While we waited in Terminal 5, he asked what work I had coming up, I listed a number of projects, and then sheepishly added, 'and then I want to finally see if I've got a book in me'. Ken's reply - 'I think you've got a lot more than one inside you' - was the spur I needed to get started, and has stayed with me to this day.

That was nearly three years ago. In the intervening period, there were a couple of moments when I was drowning under piles of research and couldn't see a way through. Ken's advice, "Don't leave it too long before you start writing," got me going again.

The bulk of the first draft was written in Australia during a sabbatical in 2011-12. I foolishly thought I'd have the whole thing finished by the middle of 2012. I learned two valuable lessons there that I pass on here to any aspiring writers. First, if you're blocking out a period of time to do some concentrated writing, then write. Don't get distracted by other work or diversionary tactics, like playing golf. Second, don't go to places that are abundant in their distractions, like Australia.

The realisation that this was going to take longer than I'd first thought, allowed me time to get some early feedback. I cannot begin to thank enough the friends who provided early critique and confidence-building: my lifelong friend Tom Kelly (who showed me how to tell stories); Mark Moorhouse (who gave me my opening paragraphs), Valerie Hannon, (who rigorously challenged some of my ideas); Rob Riordan and David Jackson (who reassured me that there would be an audience for the book, after all). I needed kind, specific and helpful feedback and they freely gave it. Later drafts were read by Mark Stevenson, to whom I owe multiple thanks since he introduced me to my agent, Charlie Viney, and provided inspiring avenues of hope through his book, *An Optimist's Tour of The Future*; and Bill Williamson (co-author of *From Exam Factories to Communities of Discovery*).

All of these people helped move me on from periodic loss of confidence to one more draft. The person who has followed the process from start to finish, however, has been my wife, Clare. She put up with my frustrations, re-assured me that I would actually get to the end, and gave invaluable support through multiple drafts. She knows how much I needed her.

Getting from drafts to publication is a tedious, though essential, journey. The Viney Agency and Crux Publishing, in the shape of the aforementioned Charlie and my editor, Christopher Lascelles, walked me patiently through each stage. I remark in the text that authors no longer *need* agents and publishers in order to write a book. That may be so for many people, but Charlie and Chris helped me to understand that going down the self-publishing route in my case would have resulted in a flabbier, less focussed and significantly delayed, final output. I'd also like to think that we're helping, in our small way, to redefine new models of partnership publishing. As part of that process, and in keeping with the theme of the book, it made sense to open up the process of the book design. My thanks, therefore, go to 99designs.co.uk - living proof of the power of disintermediation.

I'm particularly grateful to those people who generously gave their time to be interviewed: Nancy White; Matt Moore; Scott Drummond; Stephen Harris; Anne Knock; Marc Lewis; Annalie Killian; Patrick McKenna; Donnie McLurcan, and, in between rounds of golf and many laughs, Larry Rosenstock.

The idea for the book came after many years of theory postulation with friends and colleagues, and being inspired by the work of others. Sometimes it's the most casual remarks that open up a whole new line of enquiry and research, so it's impossible to list everyone who has provided me with inspiration, but mention should go to all those who have left comments on my blog (engagedlearning.co.uk), followed me on Twitter (@davidpriceobe), allowed me to watch them work, or talked to me after a presentation I gave, or a workshop I facilitated – your work has been a constant source of inspiration. Special mention should go to colleagues and friends who challenged or affirmed my hunches, either in meetings or over after-work beers. Some of them (like Stephen Sondheim and Yong Zhao) provided valuable inspiration by mail, and email. They all helped initiate, or refine, the emerging ideas that appeared in the book: Gerri Moriarty, Sugata Mitra, Matthew Horne, Ron Berger, David Hargreaves, Abigail D'Amore, Vicki Selby, Anna Gower, Laura McBain, Ben Daley, Fran Hannon, John Hogan, Ryan Tracey, Ian Clethero, Denise Scala, Margot Foster, Ken Owen, Cady Staff, Chris Wakefield, Darrick Whang, Ian Harvey, Lucy Green, Regis Cochefert, Denise Barrows, Lord Moser, Robert Dufton and all of the staff at the Paul Hamlyn Foundation and the Innovation Unit. Final drafts of the book were read by Paul Kaiserman, whose positive critique was just what I needed, and Tim Riches, who not only gave feedback, but also gave me a laptop after a second calamitous computer failure. During a period of illness, four years ago, I doubted whether it was worth starting this book, as I wasn't entirely sure I'd be around to see its completion. So, special personal thanks go to Jean Kluver, my wife Clare (again), my sister Lyn, the kind folks at various health forums, and especially to my oncologist, David Bottomley, at St James Hospital in Leeds, who made it possible to think about writing, not just this one, but the next one as well.

Finally, my biggest thanks must go to my two sons, Jack and Patrick. They not only helped me to see the urgency, and inevitability of 'Open', they also gave me invaluable source material and references to follow up. The process of writing this book has provoked feelings of thankfulness at being a baby-boomer, and guilt for the difficulties facing today's under-30s. Despite the challenges they face, I'm confident that their sense of ingenuity, generosity and morality will ensure the world is in a better place than the way we're leaving it.

COMMENTS

Comments are gratefully accepted by the author.

Please send these to educationalarts@gmail.com

For more information on OPEN, interviews, podcasts and

deleted scenes, please go to: www.open-thebook.com

Also available from

Crux Publishing

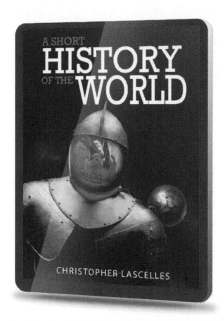

A SHORT HISTORY OF THE WORLD

"A clearly written, remarkably comprehensive guide to the greatest story on Earth - man's journey from the earliest times to the modern day. Highly recommended."

**Dan Jones, author of The Plantagenets:
The Kings Who Made England**

A Short History of the World, by Christopher Lascelles, is a short and easy-to-read ebook that relates the history of our world from the Big Bang to the present day. It assumes no prior knowledge of past events and 32 maps have been especially drawn to give the reader a better understanding of where events occurred.

The book's purpose is not to come up with any ground-breaking new historical theories. Instead it aims to give a broad overview of the key events so that non-historians will feel less embarrassed about their lack of historical knowledge when discussing the past. The result is a history book that is reassuringly epic in scope but refreshingly short in length – an excellent place to start to bring your knowledge of world history up to scratch!

223

Printed in Great Britain
by Amazon.co.uk, Ltd.,
Marston Gate.